Explorations

Explorations

A New Approach to Music Fundamentals

Second Edition

J. Timothy Kolosick
The University of Arizona

Allen H. Simon

Mayfield Publishing Company
Mountain View, California
London • Toronto

Library of Congress Cataloging-in-Publication Data

Kolosick, J. Timothy.
    Explorations : a new approach to music fundamentals / J. Timothy Kolosick,
Allen H. Simon. — 2nd ed.
    p.   cm.
    Includes index.
    ISBN 1–55934–698–1
    1. Explorations (Computer file) 2. Music—Theory. Elementary–
–Computer programs. I. Simon, Allen H. II. Title.
    MT7.K78 1997   <case MR>
    781.2—dc21   97-101
                                                CIP
                                                MN

Manufactured in the United States of America
10   9   8   7   6   5   4   3   2

Mayfield Publishing Company
1280 Villa Street
Mountain View, California 94041

Sponsoring editor, Janet M. Beatty; production editor, Julianna Scott Fein; manuscript
editor, Jamie Fuller; design manager, Jeanne M. Schreiber; cover designer, Linda
Robertson; cover art, Robin Mouat, John Waller, and Judy Waller; manufacturing
manager, Randy Hurst. The text was set in 12/14 New Century Schoolbook and
printed on 45# acid-free Baycoat Velvet by Banta Book Group.

Preface

Explorations: A New Approach to Music Fundamentals is a music learning environment that combines a music fundamentals textbook with instructional computer software. The book and the software are designed for students with no previous knowledge of music or computers.

New to This Edition

MIDI Input Capability for the Music Editor. The Music Editor now allows MIDI input into student musical compositions using a MIDI-compatible keyboard. The duration of each note is established by clicking on the Music Toolbox; then notes are placed on the staff when a MIDI key is pressed. A complete discussion of this capability is found in Chapter 4.

View MIDI Feature. In addition, a View MIDI selection has been added to the Edit Menu. This new feature allows students to see the actual MIDI data that are sent through the MIDI cables and to understand what those numbers mean. Appendix D provides a full discussion.

Expanded Written Assignment Sections. The number of written assignments for each chapter has been increased. This gives the student more opportunities to practice musical skills when not using the software that accompanies this book.

Subject areas covered in *Explorations* include the following:

Note Recognition	Rhythm and Meter	MIDI	Key Signatures
Scales	Intervals	Triads	Seventh Chords
Chord Function	Diatonic Melody	Voice Leading	

The textbook provides
- Written explanations of musical elements and relationships
- Suggested activities for exploring musical elements with the computer
- Musical scores for solo or ensemble performance
- Creative exercises as an introduction to music composition
- Written exercises to reinforce each musical topic
- Useful reference sections as appendixes to the text
- Guitar chord charts and piano fingerings for scales and arpeggios

Explorations software has the following features:
- An exploratory learning environment for each musical subject
- Practice sessions and tests to supplement written exercises in the book
- Ear training through practice sessions and tests
- Record keeping for percentage scores on music skill tests
- A Music Editor for writing assignments and musical compositions
- An online textbook and dictionary for convenient explanations of topics
- Support for MIDI keyboard entry and performance
- Tone color editing for manipulating Macintosh sound resources

Students enter musical information into the computer using three entry methods:
- Writing musical notation with the mouse directly on a musical staff
- Entering musical labels by clicking on interval names, solfège, and so on
- Playing music on a MIDI instrument or the Screen Keyboard

Explorations software is more than a set of drill and practice programs. Students explore the fundamentals of musical structure and sound and develop their own approach to learning based on a guided plan, suggested by the textbook. The textbook encourages them to experiment, to explore, increasing their curiosity about music. When students learn independently, valuable class time is available for more creative activities such as performance and improvisation.

In addition to teaching musical skills, this textbook/software combination provides an introduction to the computer skills used in today's musical world for music editing, production, and performance. For example, the *Explorations* Music Editor functions similarly to other music editing and notation programs, and in Rhythm drills students learn to play with a "click track." This approach makes *Explorations* an exciting, timely way to learn about the fundamentals of music.

For an explanation of hardware requirements and how to use *Explorations*, please turn to the Introduction.

Acknowledgments

We are grateful to those who developed the products we used to produce *Explorations*. The textbook was prepared on a Macintosh computer with PageMaker from Adobe Systems, Inc. The software was developed using Think Pascal from Symantec Corporation. It supports Sonata, a musical font developed by Adobe Systems, Inc. With the purchase of this font, users can print laser-quality musical scores with the *Explorations* Music Editor.

Our thanks go to the well-qualified and helpful reviewers of this textbook and software for both editions of this text. For the first edition review, we thank Ann Blombach, Ohio State University; Helen Brown, Purdue University; Bruce Campbell, Michigan State University; Ellon Carpenter, Arizona State University; Jane Clendinning, Florida State University; John Schaffer, University of Wisconsin; Peter Webster, Northwestern University; and Richard Wedgewood, University of Manitoba. Special thanks go to Jana Millar, Jennifer Speck, and William Bernatis of Baylor University, as well as Elizabeth Kirkpatrick of the University of Southern California, for their assistance in field testing *Explorations*.

For the second edition, we would like to thank Jane Clendinning, Florida State University; Kenneth Harrison, College of San Mateo; Ann Hawkins, University of South Florida; Tim Hurtz, Pennsylvania State University; Jana Miller, Baylor University; and Peter Webster, Northwestern University.

We deeply appreciate the efforts of Janet M. Beatty and the entire staff of Mayfield Publishing Company, especially for their willingness to use modern publication techniques in order to produce these materials. Our families, friends, and students also deserve praise and thanks for their patience and helpful support.

Contents

Introduction

Welcome to *Explorations: A New Approach to Music Fundamentals. Explorations* offers an exciting new way to learn about music by introducing you to musical concepts and allowing you to take part in guided exercises with *Explorations* software while reading.

Exploratory exercises are always indicated by a shaded portion of the page. These exercises will give you a better understanding of the material you have studied. If you do not have a computer nearby at the time, you can simply read on in the book, but don't forget to return to the exercises when a computer is available.

After your reading, you'll use the software to explore these concepts even further on your own, always asking, "What happens if...?" Such experimentation allows you to organize and compare musical concepts freely.

After you've studied and explored each concept, you'll want to double-check your understanding of it. *Explorations* software provides drill and practice to reinforce each musical skill. During a practice session, you will receive hints if you aren't sure of the right answer. Later, you can put your knowledge to the test. The computer will keep records of your progress in music writing, music analysis, ear training, and keyboard skills.

Explorations assumes no previous knowledge of music. Within each subject area you learn to write and analyze music, play musical keyboards, and develop aural skills. You have complete freedom! If you get inspired to create a new musical score, leave your present subject and start composing with the *Explorations* Music Editor. *Explorations* allows you to move freely among all areas of the software.

As you use *Explorations*, keep in mind three ways to learn each subject:

- **Read!** The textbook contains explanations that are short and to the point and will give you a good introduction to each topic. The readings will make sense on their own, but it will be helpful if you read the book with the computer software available, as this will greatly enhance your understanding of the concepts presented in the book.

- **Explore!** Start with the computer activities suggested in the book. These will demonstrate the musical concepts introduced in your reading. Then try new activities on your own. Work with musical elements and notation using the computer as a resource tool for musical learning. Try new things! Musical exploration never damaged a Macintosh! *Explorations* lets you probe the limits of each musical topic.
- **Test yourself!** Practice and test your newly acquired knowledge. Find out how much you really know. If a test score is less than desirable, further exploration and practice will increase your chances for a better score next time.

As you learn music fundamentals, remember that musical notation represents musical sounds. Whether you are working within a subject area or writing your own compositions with the Music Editor, *listen* to the sound often.

What You Need to Use Explorations

Explorations requires a Macintosh Plus computer with two 800K disk drives as a minimum system. It is also compatible with Macintosh SE and Macintosh II computers. *Explorations* supports, but does not require, a MIDI-compatible keyboard. Nonkeyboard MIDI devices such as voice trackers or MIDI guitar controllers will function properly but may require some adjustment on your part. *Explorations* also supports Sonata font from Adobe Systems, Inc. for laser-quality music printing (purchased separately).

How to Use Explorations

Explorations software uses the standard Macintosh user interface. If you are new to the Macintosh computer, read the tutorial in Appendix A of this book. It gives a detailed explanation of *Explorations* and the Macintosh. You will want to have a Macintosh available when you read and execute that tutorial.

Explorations allows your instructor to design a musical fundamentals program for your specific musical needs. Your instructor has prepared the practice sessions and tests to match the requirements of your class.

To prepare your disk for your instructor's class list, simply do the following:

1. Insert the original published disk into an available Macintosh disk drive.
2. Double-click on the *Explorations* icon.
3. When the computer asks for your name, **type carefully. Your decision is final.** The name you enter should be the same as the name you used to register for your music class. Type your first name, followed by a TAB key, and your last name.

Once your name is registered on the disk, you can begin to explore the musical subjects in *Explorations* software. For increased speed, copy the *Explorations* disk to your hard drive. At some point you may be asked to give the original published disk to your instructor in order to record your name in your instructor's computer roll sheet. Your instructor may also choose to add personalized practice sessions and tests to your disk.

After your instructor returns your disk, make a backup copy of your program on another disk. Use this copy for your daily work and keep the published disk in a safe place. As you complete tests, you will want to back up your scores. Copy *Explorations* software to your original disk from time to time in order to keep a copy of your most recent scores. Simply drag the *Explorations* icon to the other disk on the Macintosh desktop. You may choose to print your test scores periodically for a permanent record. Back up everything! Disks can and do go bad from time to time. If you have any problem with the original published disk, please contact the publisher.

The Explorations *Screen*

The *Explorations* textbook refers to various parts of the computer screen by name. The figure on the next page shows the parts of a typical *Explorations* screen. Appendix B gives a complete description of these items.

The **menu bar** displays all available menus. As you read chapters in the *Explorations* textbook, you will be asked to select items from these menus.

The **Music Toolbox** is a collection of musical symbols available to you for writing music and answering questions with musical notation. Clicking on a music symbol in the Music Toolbox changes the cursor to the appropriate shape. Clicking on a music staff with that cursor allows you to add musical symbols to your score. The Play button in the middle allows you to hear any musical score on the screen, and the Pointer Tool (shaped like an arrow) is used to select a note or a group of notes to move or delete. The Erase Tool can be used to delete individual musical items.

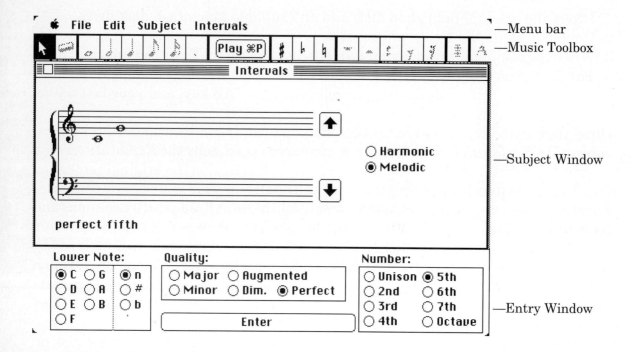

The **Subject Window** is always in the center of the screen and contains the material for the subject you have chosen at any particular session. You can request several subjects, which remain open until you close them. The musical material in the Subject Window changes depending on your activity.

The **Entry Window** is always at the bottom of the screen and is used to enter musical labels appropriate to the subject under investigation. Musical scores in the Subject Window will reflect the choices you make in the Entry Window. When you select Screen Keyboard from any of the Subject menus, the Entry Window is replaced by the **Keyboard Window**.

Above all, enjoy your *Explorations!* Learning about music is a joyful, exciting experience. Be willing to experiment and explore new areas of music learning. If some choice in the program seems unclear, simply try it out and see how the program responds. Make this learning environment work for you. Even familiar areas of music become more exciting when you explore them to the fullest.

1 *The White Keys of the Keyboard*

Knowledge of the piano keyboard is essential for learning music fundamentals, since its layout is directly related to musical notation. As you study music, regular practice on any readily available piano, organ, or synthesizer keyboard will be extremely helpful. Keyboards with full-sized keys are easier to play, but you will find smaller keyboards more portable for classroom work. (Keep your keyboard's headphones handy for working in otherwise quiet environments such as libraries.) If you don't have a keyboard available, use the screen keyboard in *Explorations* software.

As you move to the right on the piano keyboard, the sounds get higher. Moving to the left produces lower sounds. Each white key of the keyboard has a name based on the first seven letters of the alphabet (A, B, C, D, E, F, G). These letters repeat every eight white keys. The distance from any key to another key with the same name is called an **octave**.

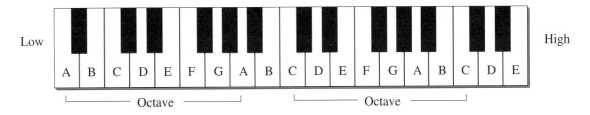

Figure 1–1

The black keys of the keyboard are found in groups of twos and threes and can be used as landmarks for identifying white keys. Each white key located immediately 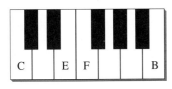 to the left of a group of two black keys is labeled C, and the white key immediately to the right of the group is called E. F keys are located immediately to the left of any group of three black keys, and B keys are to the right. The names used for black keys will be discussed in Chapter 2.

Figure 1–2

Complete the exercises for Chapter 1 that follow this page. Afterwards, use *Explorations* software to explore musical notation as an introduction to Chapter 2. Select Note Names from the Subject menu. A grand staff containing a note (middle C) along with a graphic piano keyboard will appear. (If you have a MIDI keyboard attached to your computer, select MIDI Preferences… from the Edit menu, and see Appendix D for details.)

Play the tunes in the exercises for this chapter on the screen keyboard by moving the Arrow Tool to the appropriate key and clicking the mouse button. You can also use a MIDI keyboard to play the notes. Notice how each note appears on the staff. Play the tunes in several different octaves; that is, start on a higher or lower key with the same letter name. This portion of the software notates only pitches and not the length of each note. Chapter 3 shows how to write note durations, that is, the rhythm of a melody.

Exercise 1: Practice locating white keys in the following exercises.

Write the letter C on all C keys and the letter F on all F keys on the following keyboard.

Write the letter B on all B keys and the letter E on all E keys on the following keyboard.

Write the letters D, G, and A on all appropriate keys of the following keyboard.

Exercise 2: Using only the notes marked on the keyboard below, learn to play "Twinkle, Twinkle, Little Star." Start on any C on your keyboard and figure out the other notes. Write the note name for each syllable on the lines provided on the following page.

C D E F G A

$\overline{\text{Twin}}$ - kle, $\overline{\text{Twin}}$ - kle, $\overline{\text{Lit}}$ - tle $\overline{\text{Star.}}$

$\overline{\text{How}}$ $\overline{\text{I}}$ $\overline{\text{won}}$ - der $\overline{\text{what}}$ $\overline{\text{you}}$ $\overline{\text{are.}}$

$\overline{\text{Up}}$ $\overline{\text{a}}$ - bove $\overline{\text{the}}$ $\overline{\text{world}}$ $\overline{\text{so}}$ $\overline{\text{high,}}$

$\overline{\text{Like}}$ $\overline{\text{a}}$ $\overline{\text{dia}}$ - mond $\overline{\text{in}}$ $\overline{\text{the}}$ $\overline{\text{sky,}}$

$\overline{\text{Twin}}$ - kle, $\overline{\text{Twin}}$ - kle, $\overline{\text{Lit}}$ - tle $\overline{\text{Star.}}$

$\overline{\text{How}}$ $\overline{\text{I}}$ $\overline{\text{won}}$ - der $\overline{\text{what}}$ $\overline{\text{you}}$ $\overline{\text{are.}}$

Exercise 3: Using the notes marked on the keyboard below, learn to play "Oh, Susanna." Start on any G on your keyboard and figure out the other notes. Write the note name for each syllable on the lines provided. (Some syllables use two notes; write both note names.)

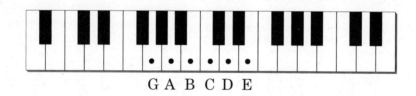

G A B C D E

$\overline{\text{Oh,}}$ $\overline{\text{I}}$ $\overline{\text{come}}$ $\overline{\text{from}}$ $\overline{\text{A}}$ - la - ba - ma $\overline{\text{with}}$ $\overline{\text{my}}$ $\overline{\text{ban}}$ - jo $\overline{\text{on}}$ $\overline{\text{my}}$ $\overline{\text{knee,}}$

$\overline{\text{I'm}}$ $\overline{\text{goin'}}$ $\overline{\text{to}}$ $\overline{\text{Lou'}}$ - si - a - na $\overline{\text{my}}$ $\overline{\text{true}}$ $\overline{\text{love}}$ $\overline{\text{for}}$ $\overline{\text{to}}$ $\overline{\text{see.}}$

$\overline{\text{It}}$ $\overline{\text{rained}}$ $\overline{\text{all}}$ $\overline{\text{night}}$ $\overline{\text{the}}$ $\overline{\text{day}}$ $\overline{\text{I}}$ $\overline{\text{left,}}$ $\overline{\text{The}}$ $\overline{\text{wea}}$ - ther, $\overline{\text{it}}$ $\overline{\text{was}}$ $\overline{\text{dry,}}$

$\overline{\text{The}}$ $\overline{\text{sun}}$ $\overline{\text{so}}$ $\overline{\text{hot,}}$ $\overline{\text{I}}$ $\overline{\text{froze}}$ $\overline{\text{to}}$ $\overline{\text{death,}}$ $\overline{\text{Su}}$ - san - na $\overline{\text{don't}}$ $\overline{\text{you}}$ $\overline{\text{cry.}}$

$\overline{\text{Oh,}}$ $\overline{\text{Su}}$ - san - na, $\overline{\text{oh}}$ $\overline{\text{don't}}$ $\overline{\text{you}}$ $\overline{\text{cry}}$ $\overline{\text{for}}$ $\overline{\text{me,}}$

$\overline{\text{For}}$ $\overline{\text{I}}$ $\overline{\text{come}}$ $\overline{\text{from}}$ $\overline{\text{A}}$ - la - ba - ma $\overline{\text{with}}$ $\overline{\text{my}}$ $\overline{\text{ban}}$ - jo $\overline{\text{on}}$ $\overline{\text{my}}$ $\overline{\text{knee.}}$

Exercise 4: Choose from the following list of melodies. Write out the words (if you know them) and the letter name of each note, as in earlier exercises. Start with the given note and play the tunes on the white keys of a keyboard.

Title	Starting Note
a. Row, Row, Row Your Boat	C
b. When the Saints Go Marching In	C
c. Long, Long Ago	C
d. Silent Night	G
e. Joy to the World	C
f. Jingle Bells (chorus only)	B
g. Skip to My Lou	E
h. Reveille (military tune)	G
i. Taps (military tune)	G
j. The Alphabet Song (A-B-C)	C (Same tune as in an earlier exercise!)

Exercise 5: Play the following notes on a keyboard and write the name of each resulting tune. When the melody changes letter names, play the *nearest* white key for the new letter name. The approximate length of each note is shown by the amount of space that follows it. The letter names represent only the opening portion of each melody. Some are folk songs and popular tunes, while others are famous classical pieces. Some of these compositions may not be familiar to you. Try to identify as many as you can. (The answers are given on the following page.)

Notes	Song Title
a. G G E G A G E E D E D	_____
b. E E G E E G E G C B A A G	_____
c. C E E E D E F E E D D D C D E C	_____
d. E D C D E E E D D D E G G	_____
e. C C D B C D E E F E D C	_____
f. F B C F B C D B C D B C	_____
g. E G G E D C D E G E D	_____
h. C D E C C D E C E F G E F G	_____
i. G G A G C B G G A G D C	_____
j. E E F G G F E D C C D E E D D	_____

Answers to Exercise 5:

    a. Camptown Races
    b. Brahms Lullaby
    c. The Bear Went Over the Mountain
    d. Mary Had a Little Lamb
    e. My Country 'Tis of Thee (America)
    f. "Maria" from West Side Story
    g. "Largo" from the New World Symphony (Goin' Home)
    h. Are You Sleeping?
    i. Happy Birthday
    j. "Ode to Joy" from Beethoven's Ninth Symphony

2 *Musical Notation*

To take part in the computer activities for this chapter, load *Explorations* software and select Note Names from the Subject menu. The windows shown below appear on your Macintosh screen. All terms associated with this subject and its computer screen are explained in this chapter. Use this diagram as you read.

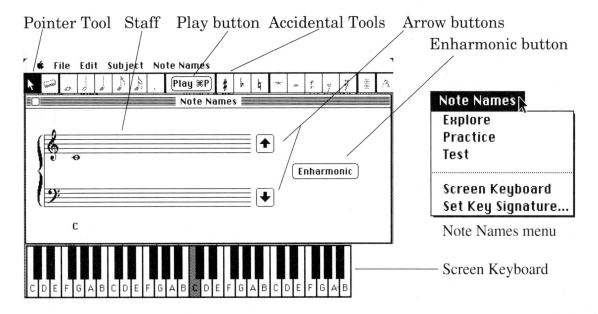

When you select this subject, a note (middle C) appears on a grand staff, and its piano key is shaded on the Screen Keyboard. You may move this single note by dragging it with the Pointer Tool or add accidentals with the Sharp, Flat, and Natural Tools. The name of each new note is written below the staff. You may set a key signature, using the Set Key Signature… item in the Note Names menu. The Up Arrow and Down Arrow buttons in the Subject Window move the note up or down by staff position within the current key signature. You may close the keyboard by selecting Screen Keyboard from the Note Names menu and request individual notes by name in the Entry Window (not shown).

When you click on Screen Keyboard to enter notes, *Explorations* software will write one suggested spelling for each piano key. The Enharmonic button in the Subject Window allows you to see different spellings for the same piano key.

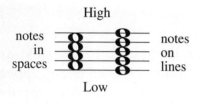

Figure 2–1

Musical notes are written on a group of five lines called a **staff** (plural: **staves**). Each line or space between lines is called a **staff position**. Notes "on a line" have a staff line running through them. Notes "in a space" are positioned between two lines.

The specific sound associated with each note is called the **pitch** (see Appendix C). Higher pitches (played on keys toward the right side of the keyboard) are written on higher staff positions, and lower pitches (played on keys toward the left side of the keyboard) are written on lower staff positions.

The first seven letters of the alphabet (A, B, C, D, E, F, and G) are used to label the lines and spaces. A **clef** on each staff determines the general range of the notes written on that staff. Clefs also establish the specific relationship between letter names and staff positions. The most common clefs, treble and bass, are shown in Figure 2–2. The treble clef is generally used in notating the upper half of the piano keyboard (the higher notes), and the bass clef is used for the bottom half (the lower notes). Verbal phrases, such as those in Figure 2–2, can help you memorize the names of the lines and spaces. Read these phrases from the bottom up, noting that the first letter of each word is the name of the line or space. After some practice these note names will become automatic.

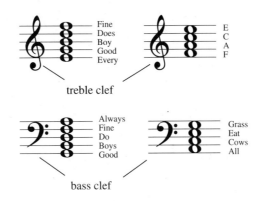

Figure 2–2

Notes that are too high or low for a staff and its clef are written using a different clef or by using **ledger lines**. Ledger lines temporarily add lines and spaces to the staff. Figure 2–3 shows ledger lines and their letter names for bass and treble clefs.

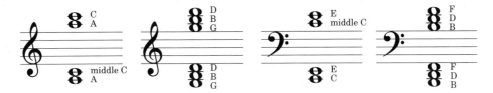

Figure 2–3

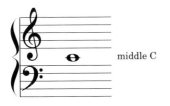

Figure 2–4

When two staves with treble and bass clefs are combined, they form a **grand staff**, as shown in Figure 2–4. The note shown in the middle of the staff is called **middle C**. The upper part of the grand staff is called the treble staff and the lower part, the bass staff.

Explore musical notation in the Note Names subject by moving the single note on the grand staff and observing the written note names below the staff. To move the note, click on the Up and Down Arrow buttons or drag the note with the Pointer Tool from the Music Toolbox. Notice how ledger lines are used above and below staves when necessary.

For every staff position there is a white key on the keyboard. Both white keyboard keys and staff positions use the first seven letters of the alphabet (A, B, C, D, E, F, G) as labels. Figure 2–5 shows notes on treble and bass staves and the portion of the keyboard they represent. Notice the position of middle C on a ledger line in both clefs.

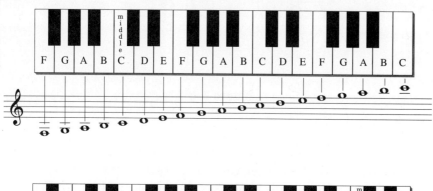

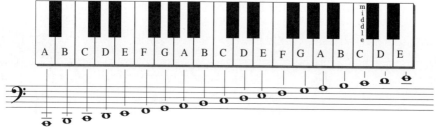

Figure 2–5

When we add ledger lines in the middle of the grand staff, we can notate several notes in two different ways. Each pair of notes in Figure 2–6 is played on the same piano key.

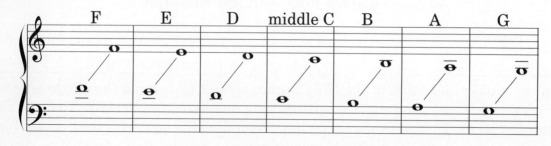

Figure 2–6

Half Steps

The distance between any two notes is called an **interval**. The smallest interval in tonal music is the **half step**. A half step is the distance between any two adjacent keys of a piano keyboard, regardless of their color. Half steps occur most often between black and white keys, but half steps between two adjacent white keys occur between E and F and between B and C. No black keys are present between white keys in these locations. Examples of some half steps are shown on the keyboard in Figure 2–7.

Figure 2–7

> Play the keys shown in Figure 2–7 on your MIDI or screen keyboard in both ascending and descending order. Observe how these keys are notated. The symbols added to the notes are called accidentals.

When **accidentals** are added to the left of a note, they change the keyboard key we use to play that note and make the sound higher or lower. The most common accidentals are **flats**, **sharps**, and **naturals**, shown in Figure 2–8. Study each accidental's shape and its placement on the staff. In Figure 2–8, practice drawing each accidental to the left of the third and fourth note in each group.

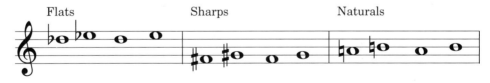

Figure 2–8

How accidentals alter a note's keyboard key and sound:

Flat (♭)   1) Note is played one key to the left.
                  2) Flat lowers the sound one half step.
Sharp (♯)   1) Note is played one key to the right.
                  2) Sharp raises the sound one half step.
Natural (♮)   1) Note is played on the white key associated with its staff position.
                  2) Naturals are used to cancel flats and sharps.

Enter an F above middle C in the first space of the treble staff using your keyboard, or move the existing note with the Pointer Tool. (The result should be the first note in Figure 2–9.) Click on the Play button to hear that F.

Click on the Sharp Tool (♯) in the Music Toolbox. Place the center of the sharp cursor in the space to the left of the note and click the mouse. A sharp appears to the left of the note (see second note in Figure 2–9). Click on the Play button and hear how the note sounds higher. The keyboard key used to play this note has also changed.

Click on the Natural Tool (♮) in the Music Toolbox. Position the center of the natural cursor in the space to the left of the note and click the mouse. The note now appears without an accidental because the sharp was canceled by the natural. Click on the Play button to hear that the note has returned to its original sound.

Choose the Flat Tool (♭) from the Music Toolbox. Place the round part of the flat cursor in the space to the left of the note and click the mouse. Click on the Play button and hear how this note sounds lower. Notice that the key used to play F♭ is the white key one half step below F. Cancel this flat with the Natural Tool.

When the Natural Tool is used to cancel these accidentals, a *written* natural does not appear on the screen. It is necessary to write the natural next to a note only in certain cases. See *Creative Exercises* at the end of this chapter.

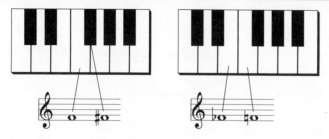

Figure 2–9

All notes with naturals are most often written without any accidental present and are all played on white keys of the keyboard. Notes with sharps and flats are played most often on black keys. Some notes with accidentals, such as E♯, B♯, F♭, and C♭ are played on white keys.

Although single accidentals (flats, sharps, and naturals) are the most common, you will encounter **double accidentals** from time to time. **Double flats** and **double sharps** alter notes in the following ways.

How double accidentals alter a note's keyboard key and sound:

Double Flat (♭♭)   1) Note is played two keys to the left.
                   2) Double flat lowers original sound two half steps.
Double Sharp (×)   1) Note is played two keys to the right.
                   2) Double sharp raises original sound two half steps.

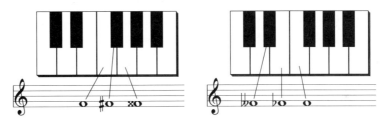

Figure 2–10

Start with an F (first space, treble staff) and click the Play button. Place a sharp to the left of the note. The screen keyboard shows the new key used to play the note. Listen to the resulting higher sound. Place the Sharp Tool over the existing sharp on the screen, and click the mouse again. A double sharp appears (see the third note in Figure 2–10). Click the Play button and hear how the sound was raised one additional half step. Now do the same exercise clicking twice with the Flat Tool from the Music Toolbox and observe how double flats lower the note's sound (compare your notes with Figure 2–10).

Any two notes that are played on the same piano key are called **enharmonic** notes. For example, D♯ and E♭ are enharmonic notes, as are E and F♭. Each keyboard key has two or three possible spellings, as shown in Figure 2–11. Don't be alarmed at the number of possible note spellings. Quick response to musical notation is simply a matter of practice. Flats, sharps, and naturals are the accidentals used most often. You will encounter double accidentals much less often.

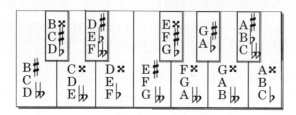

Figure 2–11

> Click on the Enharmonic button in the Note Names window. Each time you click the button, a different spelling of the same keyboard key appears. Try this with different notes on the staff. Play each spelling to hear that the sound is the same.

The spelling of each note in a composition depends on its musical context. In later chapters you will learn about the contexts that determine note spellings.

Whole Steps

Two adjacent half steps form a whole step (see Figure 2–12). For example, from A to B there are two half steps (A to A♯ and A♯ to B), which form one whole step. E to F♯ and D♭ to E♭ are two more examples of whole steps (see Figure 2–12).

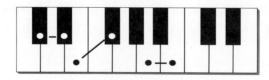

Figure 2–12

> Play the notes shown in Figure 2–12 on your MIDI or screen keyboard in ascending and descending order and observe their notation. Listen carefully to their sound.

Familiarity with musical notation and keyboard layout is very important for music study. These first steps to music literacy should be practiced daily. Recognizing note spellings, half steps, and whole steps quickly is an essential skill for recognizing and playing more complex musical structures.

Summary

1. Notes are written on the lines and in the spaces of a five-line staff.
2. Clefs determine the range of a staff and the letter names associated with staff positions. The first seven letters of the alphabet are used to label staff positions and white keyboard keys.
3. A half step, the smallest interval, is the distance between any keyboard key and the next key, regardless of key color.
4. Accidentals change the sound of a note and the keyboard key used to play it. Sharps raise a note one half step, while double sharps raise a note two half steps. Flats lower a note one half step, and double flats lower a note two half steps. Naturals cancel all accidentals for a note.
5. A whole step is equal to two half steps.

Music for Performance

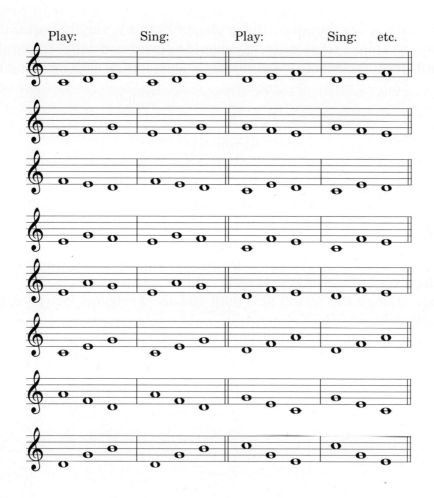

Creative Exercises

Using *Explorations* software, select New Score from the File menu and choose five grand staves by clicking on the OK button. Click on the Whole Note Tool.

Enter seven whole note B's on the middle line of the treble staff as shown below. Distribute these notes across the entire staff, leaving plenty of room between notes.

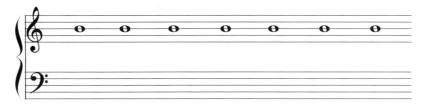

Click on the Flat Tool in the Music Toolbox and add a flat to the second note. This flat causes all six remaining notes to be one half step lower than the first note. Click the Play button to hear this example.

Add a double flat to the third note by clicking with the Flat Tool once to the left of the note. Now add a natural to the fourth note and click the Play button. Notice again that the remaining notes in the line are affected by this natural.

Click on the Sharp Tool and add a sharp to the fifth note and a double sharp to the sixth note. After the sixth note, add a barline with the Barline Tool. Notice that the computer adds a natural to the final note because the barline would cancel that accidental. Add a natural to the last note and play this example.

An accidental is active until a barline is reached. Barlines cancel these accidentals. However, when a note with the same letter name appears immediately after a barline, composers and music editors generally add a "courtesy accidental" to ensure that performers know that the accidental really should be canceled.

Click in the close box of your score (no need to save your changes to the score) and select Open Score... from the File menu. Choose Chromatic Melody from the Scores folder. Play this score and notice how the melody—the notes found on the top staff—descends by half steps. Notice the accidentals used to notate this example.

Practice and Tests

There are three types of written activities for practicing and testing the names of the notes. There are no ear-training exercises for this subject.

When you select Practice from the Note Names menu, you will see a list of activities. All types of activities for which there are tests are marked. You can choose from the available activities or you may click on the New button and design your own exercise. Choose the parameters for your drill, including clef types, note types, and activity type. Activities that you design are not stored on the disk.

Practice sessions will help you find the correct answers. Tests give no such help and simply move on to the next question. As with all practice sessions and tests, the computer will normally wait after your correct answer until you click on the Next button. You may change this by selecting Preferences... from the Edit menu and selecting the appropriate check box. Tests normally beep when answers are incorrect. This can be changed with the Preferences... dialog as well.

Write Music practice sessions and tests require you to recognize the keyboard key used to play a note. After you recognize it, you must notate that key in the correct octave on the musical staff. The keyboard key with C written on it is middle C. When you are finished notating the note, click the Ready button. If you make a mistake, move the note with the Pointer Tool or change the accidental before clicking on the Ready button or simply click on the Start Over button and begin your notation again.

In **Analyze Music** practice sessions and tests, you recognize a note on the staff and enter its correct name and accidental in the Entry Window. After clicking on the necessary radio buttons, double-check your work and click on the Enter button.

Keyboard practice sessions and tests request that you recognize a note on the staff and click on the screen keyboard key used to play that note (or press the correct MIDI keyboard key). The keyboard key with C written on it is middle C.

Exercise 1: Write the note that corresponds to the letter name given below each staff. Write the note in any octave, as shown in the first example.

Exercise 2: Write the note that corresponds to the letter name given below each staff. Write the note in all octaves, using up to two ledger lines above and below each staff, as shown in the first two examples.

D	G	C	F
F	A	D	G
G–flat	C–sharp	D–flat	F–sharp
F–flat	G–sharp	C–flat	A–sharp
F–dbl. sharp	A–dbl. sharp	E–dbl. flat	B–dbl. flat
A–dbl. flat	B–dbl. sharp	D–dbl. flat	G–dbl. sharp
F–sharp	G–flat	C–flat	G–dbl. sharp
C–dbl. sharp	G–sharp	C–dbl. flat	A–sharp

Exercise 3: Write the letter name of each note written on the staves below. If an accidental is present, write the full name of that accidental as part of your answer (for example, B–flat).

Exercise 4: Write the letter name and accidental of each note. Draw a dot on the keyboard key used to play each note, as shown in the first example.

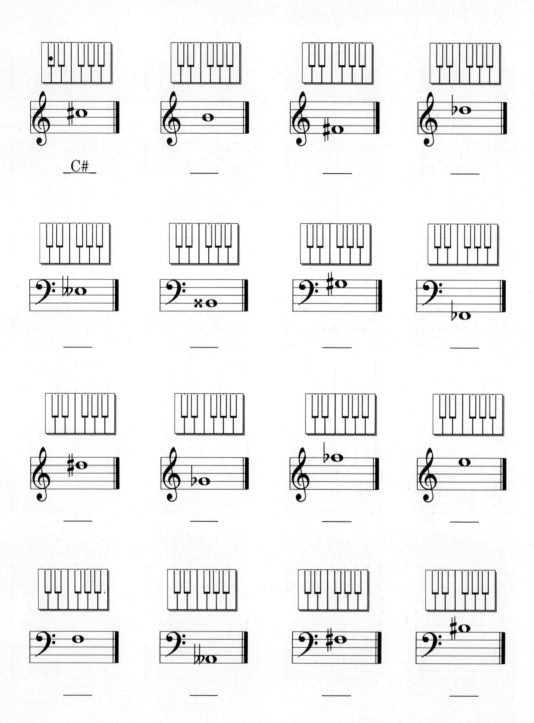

C#

Exercise 4: (continued)

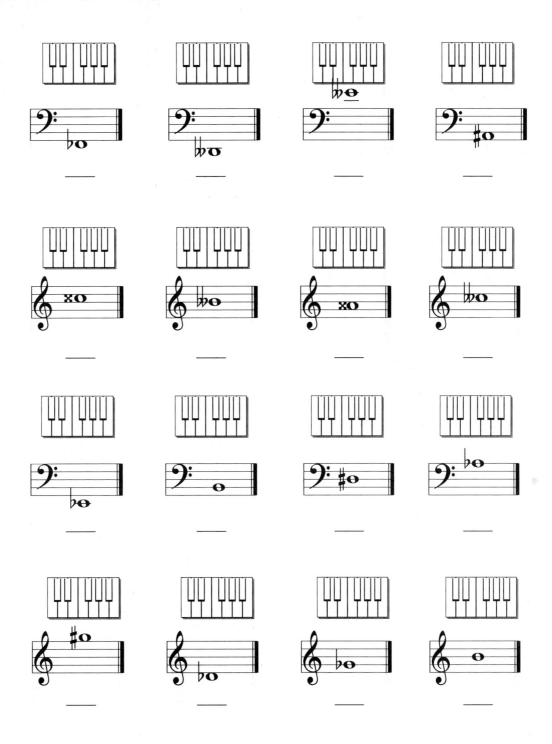

3 *Rhythm and Simple Meter*

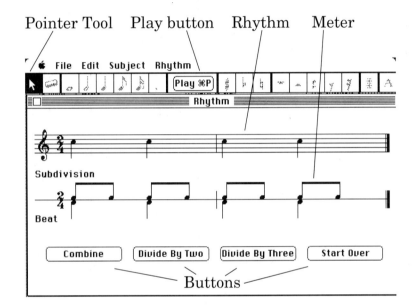

Pointer Tool   Play button   Rhythm   Meter

Buttons

Rhythm menu

In order to explore this chapter, select Rhythm from the Subject menu. The Rhythm subject starts by displaying two lines of music. The bottom line contains the metric structure, which you can hear in the varied clicks of the metronome. The top line displays a group of notes that can be changed to compose new rhythms. You can drag the notes to new staff positions using the Pointer Tool. Click with the Pointer Tool to select individual notes, or drag with the Pointer Tool to select groups of notes. When notes are selected, appropriate buttons will become available.

The Combine button combines notes into a single note value, using an acceptable notation for the longer note. Divide By Two and Divide By Three buttons divide each selected note into smaller values and notate them properly. The Start Over button returns the screen to the original state for each meter.

The items in the middle section of the Rhythm menu are identical to those in the Compose menu, discussed in Appendix B, *Using the Music Editor*. These middle items appear only during written practice sessions and tests. Explore meters by selecting Set Time Signature... and select Tempo... to make meters faster and slower. When you click the Play button, the computer plays the rhythmic melody and the metronome, repeating these measures until you click the Stop button. The metronome's lowest tick is always the first beat of each measure.

%

Musicians use note values to indicate the **duration** of a note, that is, the length of time a note should be played. When no pitches are played or sung, **rests** are used to represent durations of musical silence. Notes and rests are **rhythmic symbols**, the most common of which are shown in Figure 3–1. **Rhythm** is the set of relationships between note and rest durations in a musical composition.

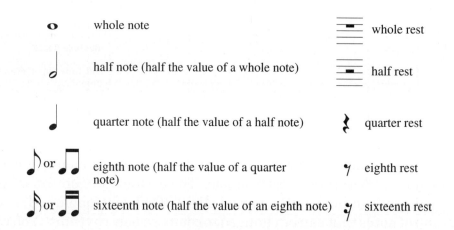

Figure 3–1

Notice that Figure 3–1 shows two symbols for representing notes that are shorter than quarter notes. Single eighth and sixteenth notes are written with **flags**. Two or more eighths or sixteenths in succession are often combined with a **beam**.

Rhythmic symbols represent the *relative* durations of notes. These ratios are shown in Figure 3–2. Rhythmic symbols operate like fractions; for example, from the top of Figure 3–2, each symbol indicates a note length that is half the duration of the previous larger value.

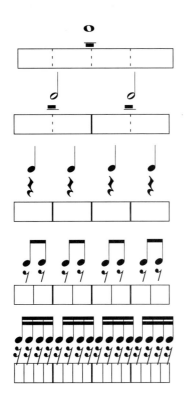

Figure 3–2

Select New Score from the File menu. Choose five grand staves by clicking OK. Write the series of notes found in Figure 3–3 on the screen by clicking on Note Tools, moving each Note Tool to the correct staff position, and clicking the mouse. Leave plenty of space between the notes. Click the Play button and notice that each type of note is twice the duration of the previous note type. Select Tempo… from the Compose menu and type 100 in the text box (tempo will be discussed later). This increases the number of quarter notes per minute and thus makes the notes happen more quickly. However, the note symbols still have the same *relative* values.

Add rests to the score to make it look like Figure 3–4. If you have placed your notes too close together, drag them farther apart with the Pointer Tool. Click the Play button to hear this score.

Figure 3–3

Figure 3–4

Two important symbols, **dots** and **ties**, help musicians establish more specific values for notes. A dot to the right of a note increases its value by one-half.

Close the score you entered in Figure 3–4 (no need to save it to disk) and again select New Score from the File menu. Choose five grand staves by clicking OK. Write the score shown in Figure 3–5, taking care to line up the notes vertically as shown. Enter a dotted quarter note by clicking on the quarter note followed by the dot in the Music Toolbox. Click on the staff with this value. After you have entered all the notes, click the Play button to hear this example. Notice that quarter notes take up the same amount of time as two eighth notes. When a dot is added to a quarter note, it takes up the time of three eighth notes. Experiment with other dotted values by writing and playing them.

Figure 3–5

Another way to make notes longer is to combine several note values using **ties**. The notes are played starting with the first note, and the sound is held through the values of all tied notes. Of course, all tied notes must have the same pitch. Be careful not to confuse ties with **slurs**. Slurs indicate smooth playing of notes with different pitches (legato).

Close the score you wrote in Figure 3–5 (don't save the changes) and select New Score from the File menu, choosing a score with five grand staves. Write the musical score found in Figure 3–6, starting by writing all the notes. Click on the Play button to hear this example. To add ties, first select a pair of notes. With the Pointer Tool, start above and to the left of the first note, and drag to the right and down until you have drawn a box around both notes. Then select Tie Notes from the Compose menu. Repeat this process for each pair of notes. Listen to this example with ties.

Figure 3–6

Tempo

The basic pulse in a musical composition is called the **beat**. This regular beat is constantly in the background of the music and guides our actions while dancing, marching, or simply clapping to the music. The speed of the beat is called the **tempo** of a composition.

Close the music score from Figure 3–6 and select Open Score… from the File menu. Open "Oh, Susanna" from the Scores folder. Click on the Play button and tap your foot to the beat of the tune. You will probably tap your foot every time a quarter note value passes.

Select Tempo… from the Compose menu. Notice that there is a quarter note on the left and the number 60 on the right. This means that sixty quarter notes occur each minute. Type the number 100 to replace the 60 and click OK. Click on the Play button and tap your foot to this new and faster quarter note beat.

Select Tempo… again from the Compose menu and quickly click on the right arrow of the scroll bar under the quarter note. This changes the quarter note to a half note and sets the tempo such that one hundred half notes occur every minute. Musicians say that the half note "gets the beat." Click OK. Click on the Play button and tap your foot to the new beat. You'll find it easier to tap your foot twice each measure rather than four times. Notice that the notation of the melody has not changed; only the speed at which the notation is turned into music has been altered.

Select Tempo… from the Compose menu. Replace the 100 with 40 and click twice on the left arrow of the scroll bar under the half note. This will change the half note to an eighth note. Now forty eighth notes will occur each minute. At this tempo, the eighth note gets the beat. Click OK. Click on the Play button and tap your foot to the new beat. Now the piece is very slow, and you tap your foot eight times per measure, a tempo that makes "Oh, Susanna" sound quite sad. To make it sound even more mournful, add a flat to every E and A in the melody. These flats put "Oh, Susanna" in the Minor Mode (see Chapter 6). Click on the Play button to hear it.

Composers specify tempo in two ways. A general way is by such words as *allegro* or *andante*, which describe the character of a composition. A more specific method is to write a metronome marking, such as those found in Figure 3–7. Metronome markings show a note value and how many such values will occur in one minute.

$$♪ = 70 \qquad ♩ = 120 \qquad 𝅗𝅥 = 60$$

Figure 3–7

Simple Meter

Meter is a musical system for organizing beats into **measures**. These measures or **bars** are indicated by vertical lines through the staff called **barlines**.

Each type of meter divides a measure into a certain number of beats. Simple meters can be **duple** (two beats per measure), **triple** (three beats per measure), or **quadruple** (four beats per measure).

Musicians show organization of the beat by using **time signatures**, consisting of two numbers. The lower number indicates the rhythmic value to be organized and the upper number shows the number of such rhythmic values in each measure. Figure 3–8 shows some of the most common time signatures for simple meter and their meanings.

$\frac{2}{4}$ = 2 ♩'s per measure $\qquad$ $\frac{2}{2}$ = 2 𝅗𝅥's per measure

$\frac{3}{4}$ = 3 ♩'s per measure $\qquad$ $\frac{3}{2}$ = 3 𝅗𝅥's per measure

$\frac{4}{4}$ = 4 ♩'s per measure

Figure 3–8

In simple-meter time signatures with moderate tempos, the upper number shows the number of beats per measure and the lower number shows the note that gets the beat, as in the following example:

$$\begin{matrix} & & \text{2 beats per measure} & & & & & \text{3 beats per measure} \\ \mathbf{\frac{2}{4}} & = & & & & \mathbf{\frac{3}{2}} & = & \\ & & \quad = \text{ one beat} & & & & & \quad = \text{ one beat} \end{matrix}$$

> Select Rhythm from the Subject menu. Exploring this subject allows you to view various meters and write rhythms in those meters. The subject opens with 2/4 meter. The top line shows a rhythm and melody, which you can change, and the lower line shows the beat and its subdivision. Click on the Play button to hear these lines played. The music will repeat until you click on the Stop button.
>
> Click on the second note head in the first measure to select it and click on the Divide By Two button. This quarter note becomes two eighth notes. Play this example. Click on the second of these two new eighth notes and click on the Divide By Two button. Two sixteenths appear. Play this example. Drag over the note heads of the eighth note on beat 2 and the first sixteenth note. Click on the Combine button. Play this example again. Experiment with other divisions and combinations of notes. Notice how the computer uses the symbols found in Figure 3–1. Drag the note heads up and down the staff to change the notes. This produces a new melody.

Just as each measure is divided into beats, each time signature implies that each beat can have a specific **subdivision**. The subdivision of each beat is the way each beat is divided when note values smaller than the beat take place. In simple meters, the subdivision is duple—that is, the beat is normally divided in half when smaller values occur. You can explore subdivision by choosing Rhythm from the Subject menu. This will be explained more fully in Chapter 9.

Each time signature implies a certain meter or organization of each measure. A natural accent or emphasis takes place on the first beat of each measure, which helps us organize musical beats in our minds. In duple and triple meters, the remaining beats in each measure are considered weak beats. In quadruple meter, a secondary accent is given to beat 3. Figure 3–9 shows the standard natural accents for several simple-meter time signatures.

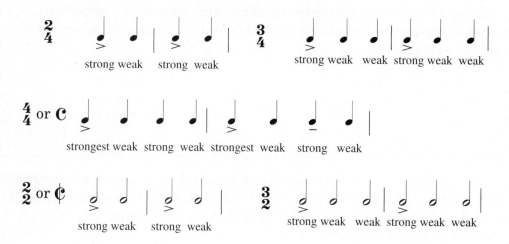

Figure 3–9

These natural accents are demonstrated by a group of musical scores on your *Explorations* disk. Although no metronome is played with these scores, the natural accents are shown by higher notes in the bass clef. Select Open Score… from the File menu and open "March" from the Scores folder. Click the Play button. This piece, like most marches, is in duple meter. A natural accent takes place on the first beat followed by a weak beat in the second half of each measure.

Select Close from the File menu; then open "Waltz" from the Scores folder and click the Play button. This piece, like all waltzes, is in triple meter. A natural accent takes place on the first beat followed by two weak beats on the second and third beats.

Open "Trumpet Tune" from the Scores folder and click the Play button. Quadruple meter is essentially two duple-meter groups per measure. The natural accent on the first beat is followed by a weak beat. On beat 3 a strong beat occurs that is not quite as strong as the first beat, followed by another weak beat.

Sometimes a composition begins with a few notes that do not form a complete measure. "Oh, Susanna," found on your *Explorations* disk, is an example of such a piece. Another example, "A-Hunting We Will Go," is found in the melodies for performance at the end of this chapter. The proper term for such extra notes is **anacrusis** or **upbeat**, but most musicians refer to them as **pickups**. A composition with an anacrusis generally has a final measure with fewer beats than specified by the time signature. Notice that in "A-Hunting We Will Go" the anacrusis is two eighth notes and the last measure is one quarter note (two eighth notes) shorter. The last measure and the anacrusis make up one complete measure.

Summary

1. The basic pulse in music is called the beat.
2. The speed of the beat is called the tempo.
3. Meter organizes beats into measures or bars separated by barlines.
4. Meters are specified by time signatures.
5. Each time signature implies a particular subdivision of the beat. In simple meters the standard subdivision is duple (by 2).
6. When a composition begins with an incomplete measure, these extra notes are called an anacrusis. Such notes are also called pickups to the first measure. The last measure of the piece and the anacrusis make up one complete measure.

Music for Performance

Rhythms

Clap, tap, or sing (any two pitches) the following exercises as a duet, with one person playing each part, or as a solo, with one person performing both parts at once (singing and tapping or tapping the parts with the left and right hands).

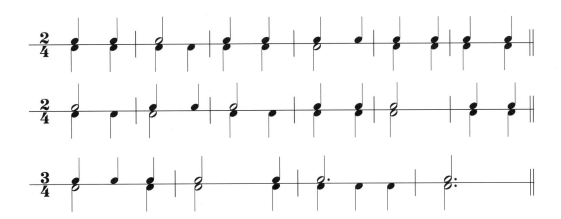

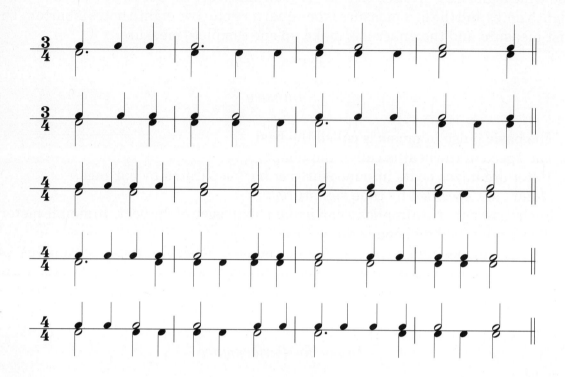

Melodies

Canon is another word for **round**. Canons are performed by groups of people who sing the same melody starting at different times. The first singer is called the **leader** and all others are called **followers**. The numbers in the score always indicate where the leader is singing when each voice starts. For example, the leader is at position 2 when the second voice begins to sing, at position 3 when the third voice starts, and so on. The fermata (often called a "bird's eye") over the last note in measures 2, 4, 6, and 8 indicates the note on which each voice should stop when the singers are ready to finish the song. All canons in this book will use this same notation.

Select Open Score... from the File menu. Select "First Canon" from the Scores folder. This is the canon "I'm a Very Happy Person," shown on the next page. Click on the Play button to hear it. Learn to sing this canon by memory. Your instructor may have you sing it alone and with other members of the class. Learn to sing your own part without getting confused when others are singing something else.

Canon: I'm a Very Happy Person

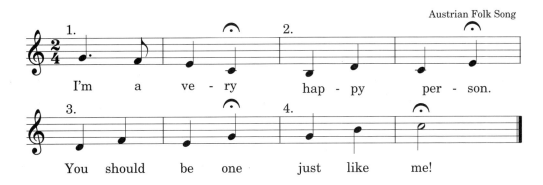

Here are two other songs for performing on your own or in class. Sing and use any instrument to play them.

America

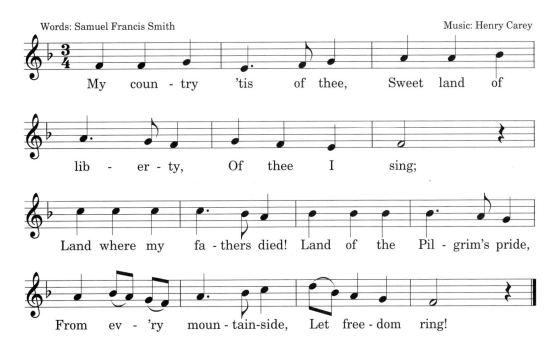

A-Hunting We Will Go

English Folk Song

Oh, a - hunt-ing we will go, a - hunt-ing we will go, we'll

catch a lit-tle fox and put him in a box and nev - er let him go.

Creative Exercises

In the Scores folder on your *Explorations* disk, you will find a file called "Ch. 3 Melody Assignment." Open that file by double clicking on its icon or by using Open Score... in the File menu. This melody is sixteen measures long and contains rhythms played on one pitch, middle C. First, save this file under a new name, using Save as... from the File menu. Using the same rhythmic values, change the notes to make a more interesting melody. Explore a variety of melodic directions: cause the melody to leap in certain places and to move stepwise in others. Stepwise movement means that the melody moves from one staff position to a neighboring staff position, up or down. You may wish to make several versions of this melody and save them to your disk. Choose the best for classroom performance.

Practice and Tests

Write Music practice sessions and tests play a rhythm and ask you to notate that rhythm using musical symbols found in the Music Toolbox. Listen carefully to each example and try to remember the entire example while you notate it. Beam eighth and sixteenth notes by selecting them with the Pointer Tool and select Beam Notes from the Compose menu. When your answer is complete, click on the Ready button.

Keyboard practice sessions and tests display rhythms on the computer screen that you play back to the computer. Click on the start button and the metronome will begin to tick. Wait until the beginning of a measure and play the rhythm on the space bar. Press the space bar when the note should begin and hold it down until the note should stop. The computer will judge your ability to play notes at the right time and to hold them the appropriate length.

Exercise 1: For each time signature below, write one measure of rhythmic values that most often represent the division of the measure called the beat. Write one measure of rhythmic values that demonstrate how beats are subdivided.

Exercise 2: In each example below, add one note with a rhythmic value that will complete the measure. For example, in the first measure a quarter note should be added.

Exercise 3: In each example below, add barlines that group the rhythmic values correctly according to the time signature.

Exercise 4: In each example below, add barlines that group the rhythmic values correctly according to the time signature.

4 *Music Notation and MIDI*

Using the Music Editor

Explorations software includes a Music Editor that allows you to write musical scores, hear them played, and print them on any printer. Selecting New Score or Open Score... from the File menu provides access to the Music Editor and adds a new menu, the Compose menu, to the menu bar. All musical scores are one page long and contain five grand staves or ten single staves. Clefs on single-staff scores can be changed by clicking on that clef *before* any notes are added to the staff. The Music Editor was designed to provide a tool for learning about musical notation and sound and does not attempt to compete with sophisticated music notation programs available today.

Compose	
Set Time Signature...	
Set Key Signature...	
Beam Notes	⌘B
Unbeam Notes	⌘U
Tie Notes	⌘I
Flip Stem	⌘F
Create Triplet Grouping	⌘R
Restore Duple	⌘D
Screen Keyboard	
Tempo...	
Keyboard Style	
Choral Style	

Compose menu

Set Time Signature... allows you to enter a time signature using a dialog box. Type the upper number of the time signature on the computer's keyboard followed by the Tab key; then type the lower number. Within this dialog, clicking the OK button will add the time signature to the beginning of the current score. The Place button allows you to place the time signature on a specific staff. To delete a time signature, click on it with the Eraser Tool.

Set Key Signature... is used to select a key signature for each system of the current score. Clicking the Entire Piece button within its dialog will add the key signature to each staff of your musical score. The Place button allows you to select a specific staff for the key signature. To delete a key signature, select Set Key

Signature… and choose C major for the entire piece or place C major on a single system.

Before the next six menu items can be used, appropriate notes in a musical score must be selected with the Pointer Tool. (For instructions on selecting notes see Appendix A - Macintosh Tutorial, Figure A-6.)

1. **Beam Notes** combines selected eighth or sixteenth notes with a single or double beam.
2. **Unbeam Notes** removes beams and reinstates flags on selected notes.
3. **Tie Notes** adds ties to connect selected notes. The notes must have the same pitch. The Music Editor will tie the notes above or below as appropriate.
4. **Flip Stem** changes the stem direction of selected notes.
5. **Create Triplet Grouping** converts selected notes into a triplet group with a proper triplet notation. This command is available only when consecutive notes have been selected whose values can form a complete triplet group.
6. **Restore Duple** turns triplet notes into duple (regular) values.

Screen Keyboard allows you to play single notes on a graphic keyboard for reference, with or without entering notes into your score. (This keyboard also enters notes within subject areas.) When rhythmic values are chosen in the Music Toolbox, the notes played are added to your musical score. To remove this keyboard from the screen, select Screen Keyboard from the menu once again. **Note to MIDI users**: You may play your MIDI instrument while exploring, practicing, or testing in any subject where the screen keyboard is appropriate. It is not necessary to open the screen keyboard to allow such MIDI entry. Just start playing. As with the screen keyboard, notes are added to your score only when rhythmic values are chosen.

Tempo… allows you to set the speed at which the Play button plays music. In this dialog you establish a rhythmic value and a number. The speed of the music is based on the number of times the selected note value occurs per minute.

Keyboard Style establishes an entry method for writing keyboard music. Notes on the same staff with identical rhythmic values are written sharing a single stem. Two different rhythmic values can occur simultaneously with separate stems.

Choral Style establishes an entry method for writing choral music. Choose the voice you wish to write or edit by clicking in one of the voice boxes to the left of the staff. These voice boxes help you establish four independent musical lines with soprano and alto on the treble staff and tenor and bass on the bass staff.

※

Musical Instrument Digital Interface (MIDI)

MIDI stands for Musical Instrument Digital Interface. For more information about this industry standard, see Appendix D.

MIDI Keyboard Entry

Explorations software allows you to enter musical notation in two ways. You can enter each note using the notation tools of the Music Toolbox, and you can play notes using the screen keyboard or a MIDI keyboard. When notes are played, they are always added to the end of a musical score.

> Select New Score from the File menu. When the dialog box appears, choose "10 single staves" to establish your musical score. You will have a musical score with ten single staves which fill a standard piece of paper. Notice that there is a treble clef on each staff. Play middle C on the screen keyboard or on your MIDI keyboard. Your score should look like Figure 4–1.

Figure 4–1

> If the notation shows any other note, double check that you are playing middle C for your MIDI keyboard. Now click on the eighth note in the Music Toolbox on the top of the screen. Play middle C again and notice that an eighth note middle C appears in addition to the previous quarter note. Click on the dot, press a MIDI key, and you will see a dotted eighth note in your score.

To enter notes into the Music Editor, choose the rhythmic value for each note (whole note, half note, quarter note, and so forth), and press the MIDI key of each note. Of course, if the rhythmic value of the notes remains the same for a while, you need not select the value for each note. Barlines and all other parts of the notation must be entered using the Music Toolbox and the mouse.

> Practice entering notes on the keyboard with the melody in Figure 4–2. For each note, click on a rhythmic value in the Music Toolbox and press the keyboard key.

Figure 4–2

Another way to select a rhythmic value for each note is to use the computer keyboard. Press the key for each value shown in Figure 4–3. The result will be the same as clicking on the Music Toolbox.

w = Whole Note	Shift w (W) = Whole Rest
h = Half Note	Shift h (H) = Half Rest
q = Quarter Note	Shift q (Q) = Quarter Rest
e = Eighth Note	Shift e (E) = Eighth Rest
s = Sixteenth Note	Shift s (S) = Sixteenth Rest
n = Natural	. = Dot
# = Sharp	| or / = Barline
b or f = Flat	a = Text Tool

Figure 4–3

Below is a second melody for practice. Try using the computer keyboard to enter the rhythmic values. Enter the time signature by selecting Set Time Signature… from the Compose menu. Enter the rhythmic values and barlines according to the chart in Figure 4–3, and enter the notes with a MIDI keyboard or with the screen keyboard. Beam the eighth notes.

Figure 4–4

You can enter more than one note at a time into the Music Editor. Find the following groups of notes and play them at the same time on your MIDI keyboard. (This is not possible with the screen keyboard.)

Figure 4–5

Synthesizer keys played while the Pointer Tool is selected are not entered into your musical score. This allows you to practice or search for notes before entering them and their rhythmic value.

Note Spellings

Musicians use MIDI in performance, composition, and education. MIDI information is really just a series of numbers. (To find out more about how those numbers are organized, read Appendix D.) The Music Editor reads the numbers that are sent from your keyboard and determines how the music should be notated.

In Chapter 2, you learned that there are three spellings for each keyboard key, except G#/Ab. When you played middle C (Figure 4–1), the Music Editor could have written that note as B#, C, or Dbb. *Explorations* bases its spelling on rules derived from musical experience and musical context. When white keys are pressed, their "natural" spelling is generally used.

Select New... from the File menu. Play the C# and E immediately above middle C, at the same time. Notice how they are notated (see Figure 4–6).

Figure 4–6

Now play that same C# key simultaneously with F. That notation is shown in Figure 4–7. This combination of notes is most often spelled as Db and F rather than C# and E#; it is almost never seen as C# and F.

Figure 4–7

As you proceed through *Explorations*, you will learn about scales and chords. These musical structures determine the common spellings of notes in combination. Pay close attention to the spellings; careful notation and common spellings make it easier to perceive and perform your notation quickly. Explore other key combinations and how they are spelled.

Musical Calligraphy

In music we use the word **calligraphy** to refer to musical symbols and how they are placed on and around the staff to produce musical scores. Rules of calligraphy are not meant to inhibit composers but to allow them to communicate their desires in a fast, efficient manner. Good calligraphy allows musicians to know immediately what the composer or arranger wants them to perform and in what manner. Today's production costs for performances, studio recordings, and musical scores force us to develop excellent calligraphy skills in order to present our ideas efficiently.

The *Explorations* Music Editor was designed to demonstrate good musical calligraphy and to help you develop scores that are easy to read. It also provides an introduction to techniques used in more sophisticated music notation programs. You can learn a great deal about the common vocabulary of musical notation by copying several short musical scores. Make your own edition of several pieces that you play or sing using the *Explorations* Music Editor or handwritten notation. Check with your local public or college library for books that give full descriptions of music calligraphy rules.

Melodies

Here are two canons and a children's song for performing on your own, in class, or with friends. Sing and use any instrument to perform them.

Are You Sleeping?

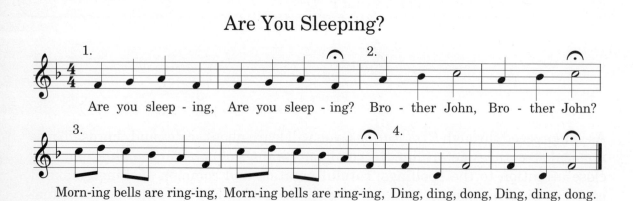

Are you sleep - ing, Are you sleep - ing? Bro - ther John, Bro - ther John?

Morn-ing bells are ring-ing, Morn-ing bells are ring-ing, Ding, ding, dong, Ding, ding, dong.

Oh, How Lovely is the Evening

1. Oh, how love - ly is the eve - ning, is the eve - ning,

2. When the bells are sweet - ly ring - ing, sweet - ly ring - ing,

3. Ding, Dong, Ding, Dong, Ding, Dong.

The Itsy Bitsy Spider

The it - sy bit - sy spi-der went up the wa - ter spout.

Down came the rain and washed the spi - der out.

Out came the sun and dried up all the rain, And the

it - sy bit - sy spi-der went up the spout a - gain.

Creative Exercises

Write a musical composition called "Train" that depicts the departure, travel, and arrival of an old passenger train with a steam locomotive. You may have ridden on such a train in an amusement park, or you may have seen one in an old film. The train would start slowly, so your composition will start with long note values. As the train gathers speed, smaller note values are used. Longer note values appear again as the train nears its next station and comes to a halt. The specific note names are completely up to you. You can choose individual pitches or groups of pitches. You may wish to use collections of pitches that sound like train whistles, screeching brakes, or a ringing bell. Use the Music Editor for your composition by choosing Open Score... from the File menu. Choose five grand staves from the next dialog box. If you have access to a MIDI keyboard, use it to enter single tones or groups of notes for this composition. Practice in order to find the sounds you want by playing while the Arrow pointer is selected. Then select rhythmic values and enter the notes. Composing with the *Explorations* Music Editor allows you to play back your composition and edit further using the mouse.

Practice and Tests

There are no specific practice sessions and tests associated with MIDI input and musical notation. All *Explorations* subjects allow MIDI input in some way. Make use of your MIDI keyboard as you learn more about the fundamental structures of music.

For practice with MIDI entry, use melodies for singing at the end of each chapter. Discover the combination of MIDI keyboard, computer keyboard, and mouse that works best for you in entering musical scores.

5 *The Major Mode*

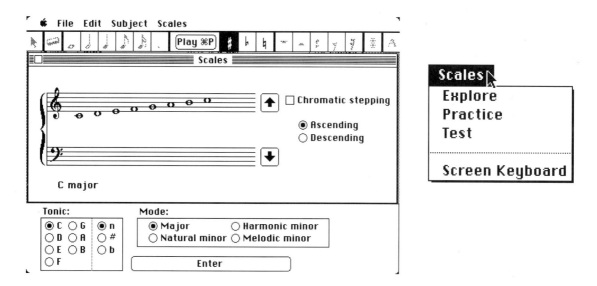

Exploring the major mode is accomplished in the Scales subject, chosen from the Subject menu. This subject opens displaying a C major scale. You can add accidentals to any note in the scale using the Accidental Tools. The Play button will play the scale. The Up Arrow and Down Arrow buttons normally move the major scale to the nearest white key note. When the Chromatic Stepping check box is checked, the scales move by half step each time an arrow is clicked. The Ascending and Descending radio buttons display the scale in ascending or descending order.

Enter a tonic and a mode and click the Enter button in the Entry Window to request any scale. The n, #, and b radio buttons represent natural, sharp, and flat.

Select Screen Keyboard from the Scales menu to enter notes through the keyboard. Click on the piano keys of the scale in their proper order. The first key you click is considered the lower tonic of the scale, or the upper tonic if Descending is selected. If your scale is a modal scale, the computer will tell you the scale's analysis. If your scale is not a common scale, the computer will respond, "Not a common scale."

This chapter also discusses key signatures. *Explorations* software allows you to explore key signatures separately from scales. Its computer screen is shown below.

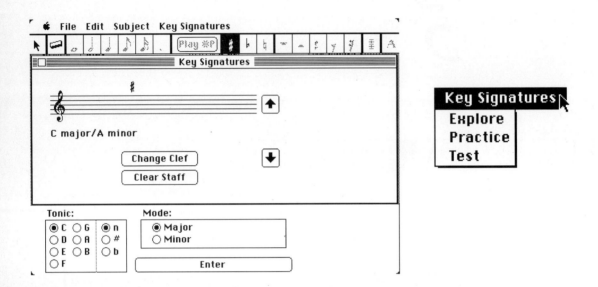

The Key Signatures subject draws a single staff for entering key signatures with a treble clef. You can alternate between treble and bass clefs by clicking on the Change Clef button. The Up Arrow and Down Arrow buttons move you through standard key signatures on the chosen clef. The Up Arrow button removes flats or adds sharps, depending on the current key signature displayed. The Down Arrow button removes sharps or adds flats. The Clear button removes all accidentals and displays the key signature for C major/A minor.

You can write your own key signatures using the Sharp Tool and the Flat Tool. Simply click on the staff with one of these tools and an accidental is added to the key signature. *Explorations* software will tell you the keys you have represented or if your key signature is not standard. You may insert new accidentals at any point in the key signature. You may not mix flats and sharps in the same key signature. Use the Pointer Tool to move accidentals around or the Erase Tool to delete them.

The Entry Window at the bottom of the screen allows you to request a key signature by selecting a major or minor key. When you press the Enter button, all the existing accidentals are erased, and your requested key signature is drawn.

𝄋

A **scale** is a series of ascending or descending notes, written on adjacent positions of the staff; it is a convenient way to show the pitches used in musical composition.

In Chapter 2 you learned that the piano keyboard is constructed with half steps between adjacent keys. There are twelve such half steps in each octave. These twelve half steps form the **chromatic scale**. Figure 5–1 shows the keyboard's layout and a common method for notating the chromatic scale on the staff. When the ascending chromatic scale is written, sharps are generally used as accidentals.

Chromatic Scale, Ascending

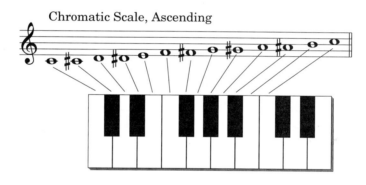

Figure 5–1

When the descending chromatic scale is written, flats are generally used as accidentals (see Figure 5–2).

Chromatic Scale, Descending

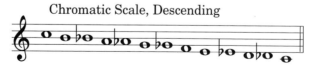

Figure 5–2

All other scales in tonal music are drawn from the notes of the keyboard's chromatic scale. The two most commonly used scales are the **major** and the **minor** scales. The notes in these scales follow established patterns of half steps and whole steps. The order and placement of these steps give the scale a particular quality that we call its **mode** (major or minor). The quality of each mode affects the overall sound of a composition. (Remember how you changed "Oh, Susanna" in Chapter 3? Those changes gave the melody an entirely new sound.)

Major Scales

The melody in Figure 5–3 is based on the notes of the C major scale. This scale is shown in the staff below the melody, with lines indicating the first appearance of each scale note in the melody. Major scales contain two half steps and five whole steps between adjacent notes. Their specific pattern of half steps and whole steps establishes the major mode. Other patterns of half steps and whole steps establish other modes (see Appendix H for a list of other modes and scale types).

W. A. Mozart: Quartet in C Major, K. 157

C major scale

Figure 5–3

Major scales are traditionally written as a series of ascending notes. In a musical composition we find notes of scales in any order and in any octave the composer finds appropriate. The movement of a melody between adjacent notes of the scale is called **stepwise** motion; a melody that moves between nonadjacent notes is said to **leap**. The melody in Figure 5–4 contains the notes of a G major scale. Notice stepwise motion and leaps in this melody. When the tones are arranged as a scale, the half steps and whole steps of the major scale are clearly visible.

J. Haydn: Symphony in G (Surprise)

Figure 5–4

Each position in the scale is called a **scale degree**. The first scale degree, or **tonic**, is the most important because it is the note that establishes key. In each written scale the tonic is duplicated at the end of the scale. The second most important scale degree is the **dominant** (5). Chords based on the dominant help establish the tonic as the tonal center (see Authentic Cadence in Chapter 13).

Using *Explorations* software, select Scales from the Subject menu. A C major scale will appear on the screen. Clicking on the Up Arrow button reveals the D major scale, clicking on the Up Arrow button a second time reveals the E major scale, and so on. Click on the Play button to hear each scale. Select Screen Keyboard from the Scales menu and explore major scales viewing the keyboard keys used to play each scale. Notice the half steps and whole steps pattern for all major scales.

Figure 5–5 compares the two major scales discussed thus far. All major scales have the same pattern of half steps and whole steps. When writing and playing major scales, remember the following points:

- Each major scale is generally written in ascending order.
- The major scale always begins and ends with the tonic note.
- Each note of the scale has its own staff position and letter name.
- Whole steps and half steps follow the pattern shown in Figure 5–5.

Major Scales

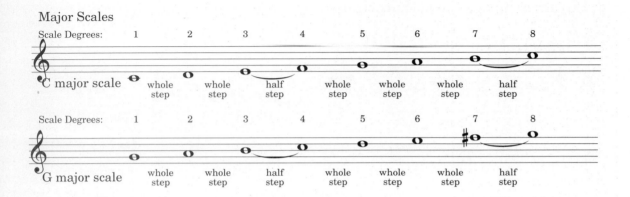

Figure 5–5

Within the Scales subject, construct some major scales using the Screen Keyboard. Start by clicking piano keys for the scales found in Figure 5–5. Enter each keyboard key in the order shown. As you complete each scale, its analysis will be provided by the computer. If you make a mistake, click on the Start Over button and begin again.

Click on the Up Arrow button to move to a new scale. After memorizing the keyboard keys for a particular scale, enter that scale by clicking on the screen keyboard or by playing on a MIDI instrument.

Keep exploring until you have a firm grasp of the half-step and whole-step pattern that makes up the major scale.

Major Key Signatures

Most major scales require accidentals on certain notes in order to establish the correct half-step and whole-step pattern. Instead of adding accidentals to these notes each time they appear in a piece, composers write accidentals in a **key signature** at the beginning of every line of music. A major key signature is a list of all flats or sharps necessary to establish a major scale. Flats *or* sharps, but not both, appear in a single key signature.

To see how key signatures work, select Open Score... from the File menu. Open the Scores folder and choose the score called "Eb Major Scale." An Eb major scale is shown on both staves. Click the Play button to hear this scale. Notice the accidentals on both tonic notes and two other pitches. Select Set Key Signature... from the Compose menu. Click on Eb major in the Key Signature dialog and click OK. When the key signature is added to the score, the individual accidentals are no longer necessary in the scale. Compare the two notation methods by selecting Undo and Redo from the Edit menu. Click the Play button to hear this new notation. Close this score (you need not save the changes), and perform the same activity with the score "B Major Scale."

The order of the accidentals is extremely important because it allows musicians to recognize immediately which key is implied. Figure 5–6 shows all major key signatures. Study the relationship between the order of accidentals and the major key tonic. Remember, no accidentals in a major key signature means C major.

Flat key signatures:
- The last flat is the fourth scale degree of the key.
- Except for F major, the next-to-last flat is the tonic of the major scale.

Sharp key signatures:
- The last sharp is the seventh scale degree (leading tone) of the key.
- The tonic is found a half step higher, on the next staff position.

These relationships can be useful tools at first, but key signature recognition should become fast and automatic.

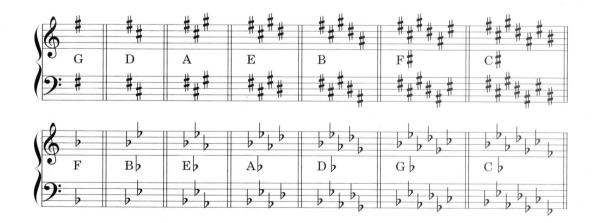

Figure 5–6

Select Key Signatures from the Subject menu. Practice the order of accidentals by entering major key signatures from Figure 5–6, using the Entry Window at the bottom of the screen, and viewing their accidentals. Click on the Arrow buttons to see the names of keys as accidentals are added or taken away. It is not essential that you understand the information given on the screen about the minor mode; these relationships will be discussed in Chapter 6. Carefully study the order of accidentals in each key signature. These must appear in the order shown and on the proper line or staff. Practice writing these key signatures using Accidental Tools from the Music Toolbox at the top of the screen.

Appendix F shows all major key signatures and their scales. Study these scales, learn to notate them, and practice them on a keyboard instrument.

Summary

1. The piano keyboard divides each octave into twelve half steps that make up the chromatic scale.
2. Musical scales are made up of notes chosen from the chromatic scale.
3. Major and minor scales are the most common tonal scales.
4. Major scales follow a series of half steps and whole steps between adjacent notes (shown in Figure 5–5).
5. Major key signatures show the accidentals necessary to establish a major key and mode.

Music for Performance

Rhythms

Clap, tap, or sing the following exercises as a solo—that is, one person performing both parts at once—or as a duet—one person playing each part.

Melodies

Select Open Score... from the File menu. Select "Rooster Canon" from the Scores folder. Click on the Play button to hear it. Learn to sing this canon by memory. Practice with others to learn to concentrate when several singers are singing different parts.

Canon: The Rooster's Dead

Austrian Folksong

1. The roo-ster's dead, oh what a shame! He on-ly has him-self to blame.

3. He crowed much too ear-ly this morn-ing, you see.

4. Now he's in the soup for my

ba - by and me.

5. Cock-a-doo-dle-doo Cock-a-doo-dle-doo-dle-doo

Here are two other songs for performing on your own or in class.

America, The Beautiful

Words: Katherine Lee Bates

Music: Samuel A. Ward

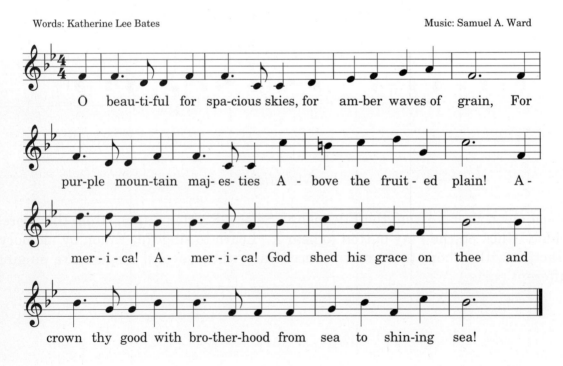

O beau-ti-ful for spa-cious skies, for am-ber waves of grain, For

pur-ple moun-tain maj-es-ties A - bove the fruit-ed plain! A-

mer - i - ca! A - mer - i - ca! God shed his grace on thee and

crown thy good with bro-ther-hood from sea to shin-ing sea!

Yellow Rose of Texas

American Folksong

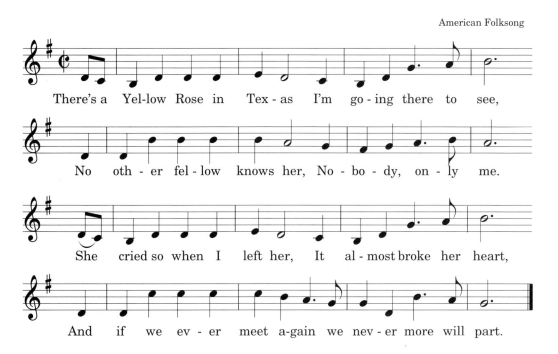

There's a Yel-low Rose in Tex-as I'm go-ing there to see,

No oth-er fel-low knows her, No-bo-dy, on-ly me.

She cried so when I left her, It al-most broke her heart,

And if we ev-er meet a-gain we nev-er more will part.

Creative Exercises

Write a musical composition that contrasts ascending and descending major scales and has plenty of action—fast notes and contrasting rhythms. Using the Music Editor available in *Explorations* software, try out some of the rhythms shown in the Rhythmic Exercises earlier in this section and experiment with a variety of tempos. The piece will probably consist mainly of individual pitches, but you can choose groups of pitches from the scales and play them together. Discover which types of sounds you like best.

Practice and Tests

There are three types of written activities and three ear-training activities for practicing and testing scales that can be used for drills with both major and minor scales. Minor scales are discussed in Chapter 6. To practice a skill or take a test, select Practice or Test from the Scales menu.

Write Music displays a scale on the computer screen or, in ear training, plays a scale and asks you to notate it. To do so, you add accidentals to a group of whole notes on the staff. Click on the necessary Accidental Tool and click to the left of the appropriate notes on the staff. Listen carefully to each scale and try to keep its sound in mind as you notate it. When you have finished your answer, click on the Ready button. In practice mode, *Explorations* software will try to help you correct problems in your musical notation.

Analyze Music shows a scale on the screen, or plays it in ear-training drills, and asks you to enter the proper label for that scale. This practice and test type is available for minor scales alone and for combination tests for major and minor scales. In the Entry Window, click on the appropriate note name and accidental for the tonic and click to the left of the appropriate notes. In ear-training drills you will not be asked to enter the tonic for the scale. When you have finished your answer, click on the Ready button. In practice mode, *Explorations* software will try to help you find the correct answer.

Keyboard practice sessions and tests display scales on the computer screen or play them in ear-training drills that you play back by clicking on the Screen Keyboard. You may also enter notes using a MIDI keyboard. When *Explorations* software receives eight notes, it will automatically evaluate your answer. In practice sessions, you will receive helpful advice that will lead you to the correct answer.

Exercise 1: Write and label major scales based on the given notes.

D major

Exercise 2: Write and label major scales based on the given notes.

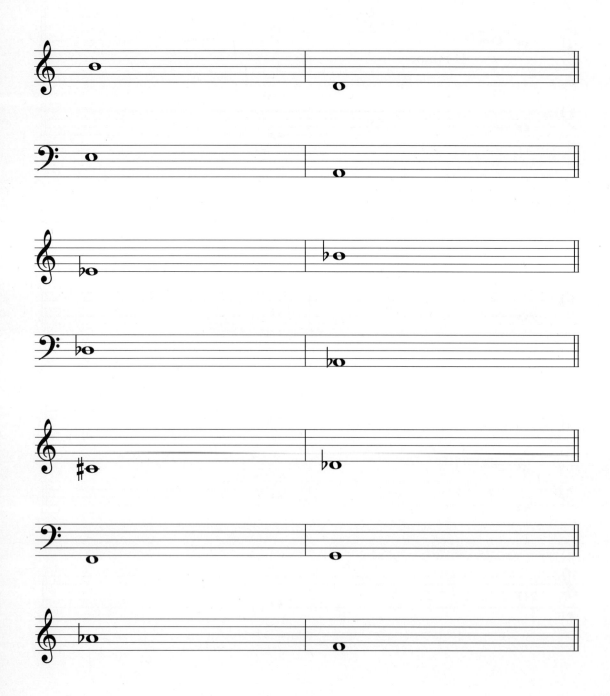

Exercise 3: Write and label major scales based on the given notes.

Exercise 4: Write the key signatures for major keys requested below.

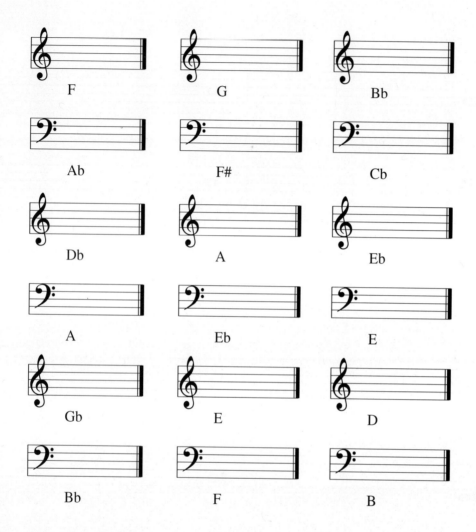

F

G

Bb

Ab

F#

Cb

Db

A

Eb

A

Eb

E

Gb

E

D

Bb

F

B

Exercise 5: Write the key signatures for major keys requested below.

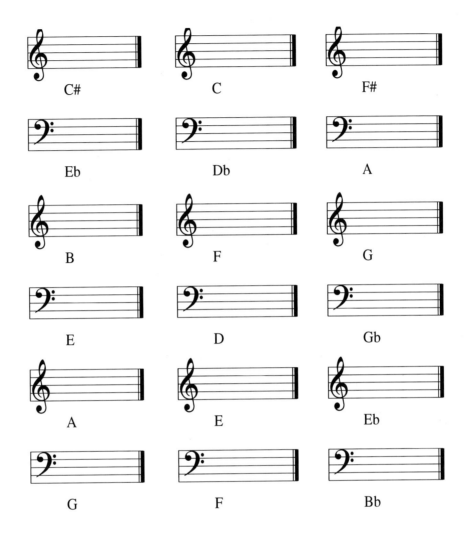

C# C F#

Eb Db A

B F G

E D Gb

A E Eb

G F Bb

Exercise 6: Write the key signatures for major keys requested below.

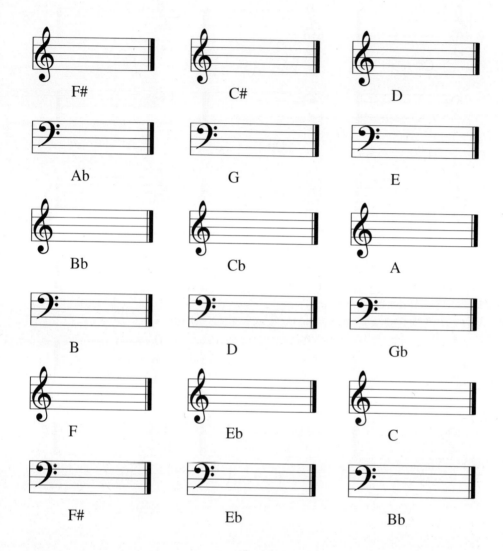

F#   C#   D

Ab   G   E

Bb   Cb   A

B   D   Gb

F   Eb   C

F#   Eb   Bb

6 *The Minor Mode*

Chapter 5 discussed major scales and their key signatures. To explore minor scales you will continue to use the Scales and Key Signatures subjects from the Subject menu. See Chapter 5 for an explanation of those computer screens.

Minor Scales

Minor scales are the second prominent type of scale in tonal music. Each minor scale has a key signature associated with it. Figure 6–1 shows the refrain of a well-known carol. The notes used in this melody are the same as the C major scale, but the final tone is A. This tonic gives the piece a sense of finality in its last measure. Play or sing this melody.

Traditional: God Rest Ye Merry, Gentlemen, Refrain

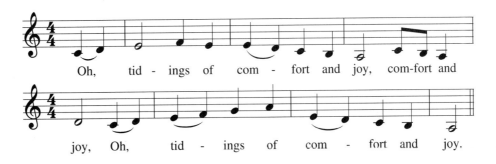

Figure 6–1

The notes of the melody in Figure 6–1 are based on the A minor scale. This minor scale shares a key signature with C major, as shown in Figure 6–2. A minor is called the **relative minor** of C major. Similarly, C major is considered the **relative major** of A minor.

71

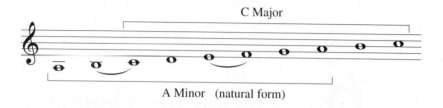

Figure 6–2

Minor scales are written in three different forms, all of which use the same key signature. The **natural minor scale** is based on the notes specified by the key signature and contains half steps between the second and third scale degrees as well as between the fifth and sixth scale degrees. All other adjacent pitches form whole steps.

Select Scales from the Subject menu. Choose A natural minor using buttons in the Entry Window and play this scale by clicking the Play button. Click on the Arrow buttons to move this scale up and down the staff. Return to A natural minor using the Arrow buttons. Choose the harmonic minor and click on the Enter button. Notice that a sharp is added to the seventh scale degree. This accidental is added to the note in the scale and not to the key signature. Choose the melodic minor and click on the Enter button. This time a sharp is added to both the sixth and seventh scale degrees. Click on the Descending button in the Subject Window. Notice that the sharps are canceled when the descending form is written. Experiment with other minor scales to see how accidentals are consistently used on the sixth and seventh scale degrees.

A **harmonic minor scale** is shown in Figure 6–3. The scale used in Bach's melody is based on C as its tonic note. Most of its notes are determined by the key signature; however, an accidental is added on the seventh scale degree. This accidental gives the minor scale a **leading tone**. A leading tone is always one half step below the tonic and is part of the key signature in the *major* mode. Its presence in the harmonic minor scale is established by an extra accidental. Notice the half steps between scale degrees 2 and 3, 5 and 6, and 7 and 8 in Figure 6–3.

J. S. Bach: Fugue in C Minor, Well-Tempered Clavier, Vol. I

C Harmonic Minor:

Figure 6–3

The harmonic minor is the basis for building chords. In the harmonic minor, the distance between the sixth and the seventh scale degrees is three half steps and is called an augmented second (see Intervals in Chapters 7 and 8). Melodies seldom use these two scale degrees to form a melodic interval.

The **melodic minor scale** has two forms, ascending and descending, which differ only in their sixth and seventh scale degrees. The upper four notes of the ascending form have the same half- and whole-step pattern as the major mode. The descending form uses the same notes as the natural minor. In Figure 6–4, Bach uses the descending form in the first part of this example and the ascending form in the remaining bars. Melodies do not always go up when using the ascending form, and they do not always go down when using the descending form. This piece can be found in the Scores folder on your *Explorations* disk under the name "Bach Partita."

J. S. Bach: Partita VI in E Minor

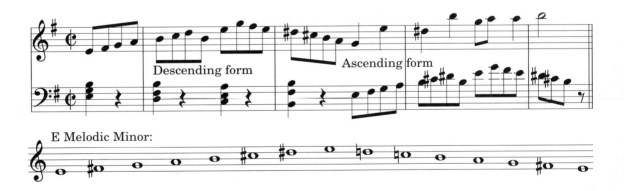

Descending form

Ascending form

E Melodic Minor:

Figure 6–4

The fifteen key signatures used in the major mode (see Figure 5–6) are also used for minor scales. Each key signature is associated with a major scale and with a minor scale. In Figure 6–2 this relationship was shown between C major and A minor, which contain no accidentals in their key signatures. You may have noticed that the C minor melody in Figure 6–3 has the same key signature as E-flat major. Figure 6–5 shows the minor key signatures along with their tonic note names. Notice that the minor tonic is always three half steps lower than its relative major. The minor tonic is the sixth scale degree of its relative major's scale. The major tonic is the third scale degree of its relative minor's scale.

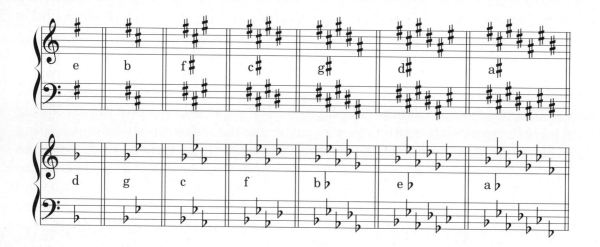

Figure 6–5

Remember: a major and a minor key that share a key signature are called the relative major and relative minor of each other—for example, C major and A minor or F major and D minor. If a major scale and a minor scale share the same tonic note (e.g., E major and E minor), they are called the **parallel major** and **parallel minor** of each other. Parallel modes never share the same key signature.

Since major and minor keys share key signatures, it may seem difficult to determine whether the minor key or the major key is represented. If you are in doubt, look at the last measure of the piece and at the lowest note in the last simultaneous group, or chord. That note is most often the tonic of the key.

Summary

1. Major and minor scales are the most prominent scales in tonal music.
2. Minor scales are written in three different forms: natural, harmonic, and melodic.
3. The natural minor has half steps between scale degrees 2 and 3, and between 5 and 6. It uses notes established by key signature.
4. To form the harmonic minor, composers raise the seventh scale degree of the natural minor, adding a half step between scale degrees 7 and 8.
5. In the ascending form of the melodic minor, the sixth and seventh scale degrees are raised; in its descending form, the tones of the natural minor are used.
6. One major key and one minor key are represented by each key signature. Two keys that share a key signature are called the relative major and the relative minor of each other.
7. Major and minor scales with the same tonic note are called the parallel major and parallel minor of each other.

Music for Performance

Rhythms

Melodies

Sample melodies from the Music for Performance sections of the remaining chapters are not included on your *Explorations* disk. Learn these melodies on your own by playing them on a musical instrument. Try to remember the particular sound of each scale degree in the three minor scales.

Canon: Hey, Ho, Nobody Home

English Folk Song

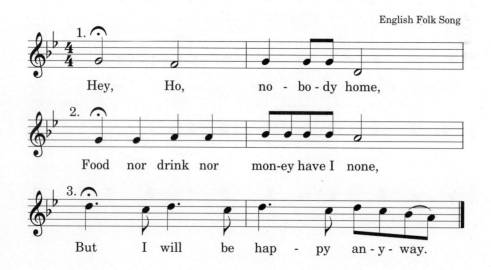

Hey, Ho, no - bo - dy home,

Food nor drink nor mon-ey have I none,

But I will be hap - py an - y - way.

Erie Canal

American Folk Song

I've got a mule her name is Sal, Fif-teen miles on the E-rie Ca-nal. She's a
good ol' work-er and a good ol' pal, Fif-teen miles on the E-rie Ca-nal. We've
hauled some barg-es in our day, Filled with lum-ber, coal, and hay, And
we know ev-'ry inch of the way From Al-ba-ny to Buf-fa-lo.
Low bridge, ev-'ry-bo-dy down, Low bridge, 'cause we're comin' to a town, And you
al-ways know your neigh-bor, You al-ways know your pal, If you've
ev-er nav-i-gat-ed on the E-rie Ca-nal.

Wayfaring Stranger

American Folk Song

I'm just a poor way-far-ing stran-ger, A-trav-'lin' through this world of

woe, And there's no sick - ness, toil, or dan-ger In that bright land to which I

go. I'm go-ing there to meet my mo-ther, I'm go-ing there no more to

roam. I'm just a- go - in ov-er Jor-dan, I'm just a- go - in ov-er home.

Go Down, Moses

Spiritual

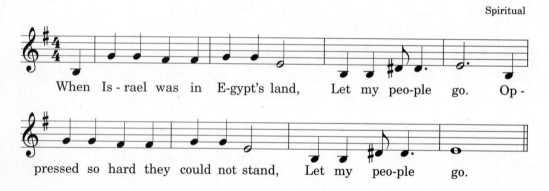

When Is - rael was in E-gypt's land, Let my peo-ple go. Op -

pressed so hard they could not stand, Let my peo-ple go.

Go down, Mo - ses, way down in E - gypt's land,

Tell ol' Pha - raoh Let my peo - ple go.

Creative Exercises

Write a "sad" musical composition, using the minor mode and a slow tempo. You may wish to use the harmonic form of the minor to give your composition a mysterious quality. If you wish, choose a sad text to set to music. It is also possible to write an amusing piece that pretends to be sad by exaggerating the slow tempo or emphasizing certain key words in the text. Review the computer activity in Chapter 3, where you changed notes in "Oh, Susanna" to produce a sad mood. Such a parody on a famous melody can produce humorous results. Use the Music Editor available in *Explorations* software to write your composition.

Practice and Tests

Written activities and ear-training drills are the same for the minor scales as for the major. Turn to Chapter 5 for instructions if necessary.

Exercise 1: Write the minor scales requested below.

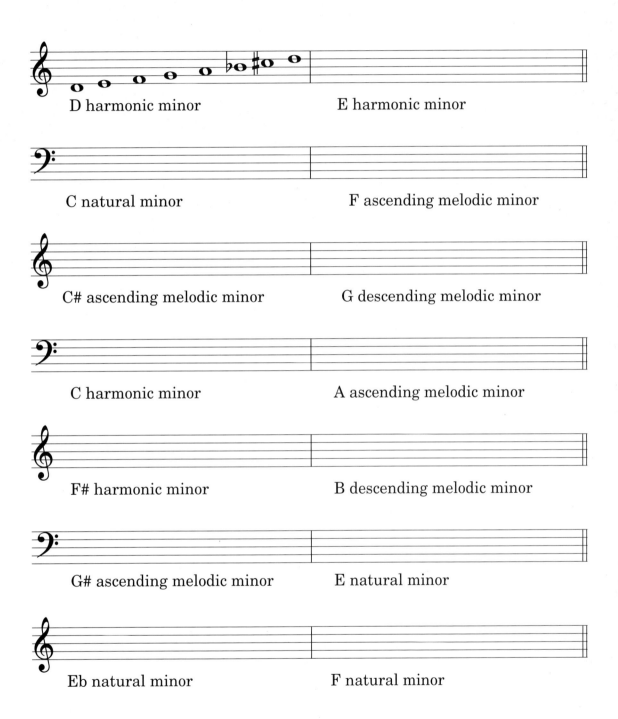

D harmonic minor　　　　　　　　E harmonic minor

C natural minor　　　　　　　　F ascending melodic minor

C# ascending melodic minor　　　　　　G descending melodic minor

C harmonic minor　　　　　　　　A ascending melodic minor

F# harmonic minor　　　　　　　　B descending melodic minor

G# ascending melodic minor　　　　　　E natural minor

Eb natural minor　　　　　　　　F natural minor

Exercise 2: Write the minor scales requested below.

D ascending melodic minor   G harmonic minor

A harmonic minor   F ascending melodic minor

E ascending melodic minor   G harmonic minor

F harmonic minor   C descending melodic minor

F# ascending melodic minor   B harmonic minor

C# descending melodic minor   G natural minor

Ab natural minor   D natural minor

Exercise 3: Identify and label the minor scales below. Write the tonic's letter name and the form of the minor, as shown in the first example.

G ascending melodic minor

Exercise 4: Identify and label the major and minor scales below. Write the tonic's letter name and the form of the minor.

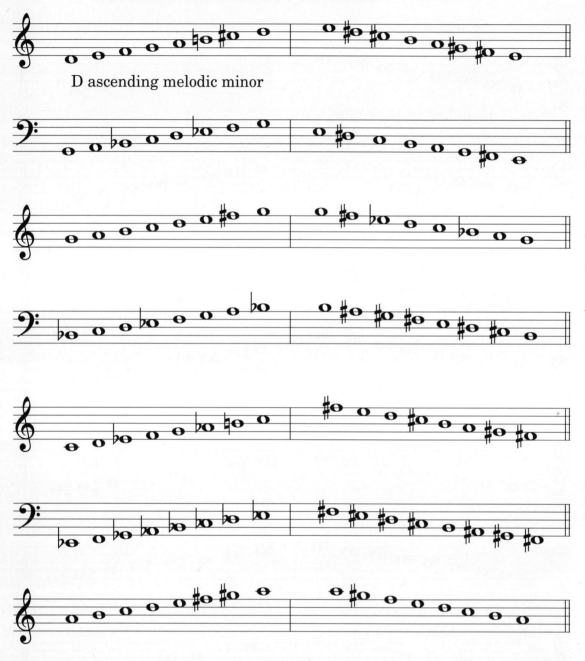

D ascending melodic minor

Exercise 5: Write the key signatures for minor keys requested below.

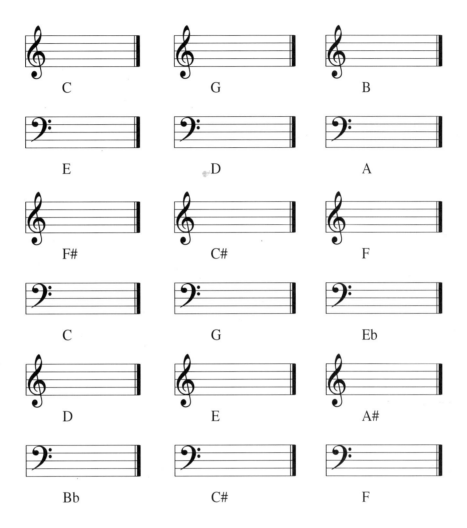

C   G   B

E   D   A

F#   C#   F

C   G   Eb

D   E   A#

Bb   C#   F

Exercise 6: Write the key signatures for minor keys requested below.

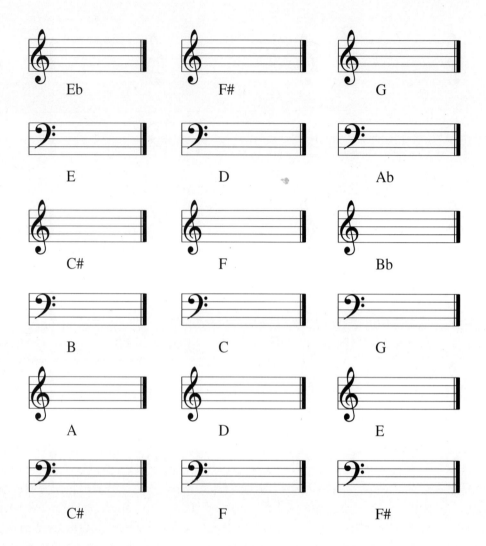

Eb   F#   G

E   D   Ab

C#   F   Bb

B   C   G

A   D   E

C#   F   F#

7 *Intervals I*

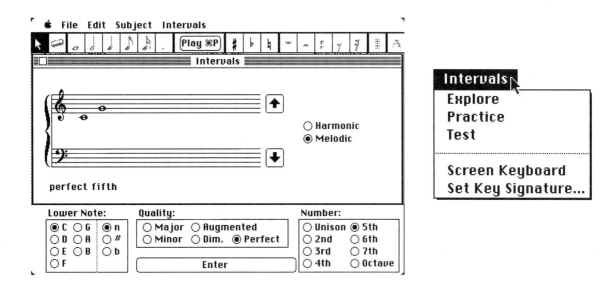

Chapters 7 and 8 use Intervals from the Subject menu. In the Explore segment, two notes appear on a grand staff. You may move the notes freely by dragging them with the Pointer Tool or move them one staff position at a time with the Arrow buttons. You can also add accidentals with the Sharp, Flat, and Natural Tools. Each time you alter a note, the new interval's label is written below the staff. You can also select Set Key Signature… from the Intervals menu and choose a new key. Observe how patterns of intervals occur within each key signature.

The Harmonic radio button presents intervals as two simultaneous notes, and the Melodic radio button writes and plays the two notes separately (melodic interval).

Use the Entry Window to request a specific interval by name. The n, #, and b radio buttons represent natural, sharp, and flat. As soon as you have chosen a lower note, a quality, and a number, click the Enter button to see and hear the interval.

Use the Screen Keyboard or your MIDI instrument to play intervals into the computer. When notes are played melodically, the first note is displayed with its name, and the second note is displayed with an interval label. Play the notes simultaneously on a MIDI keyboard and see the interval immediately.

Selecting Intervals from the Subject menu provides you with useful tools for exploring the concepts in this chapter. Select Screen Keyboard from the Intervals menu. Use this keyboard to enter notes or play your own MIDI keyboard. The Screen Keyboard will also be used to relate intervals to the layout of the piano keyboard.

An **interval** is the distance between any two notes. Interval labels describe distances between simultaneous notes (**harmonic intervals**) or between notes in a melody (**melodic intervals**). This chapter limits its discussion to intervals between members of major scales. First, we will concentrate on notes found in the C major scale, played on the white keys of the keyboard.

When the Intervals subject window appears, the Melodic button is selected. Click on the Play button in the Music Toolbox and hear the two notes played as a melodic interval. Click on the Harmonic button. Notice that the notes are written and played as a harmonic interval.

Click on the Up Arrow and Down Arrow buttons and see the notes ascend and descend on the staff. The words below the staff indicate interval labels that will be discussed in this chapter.

Each interval label has two parts: an **interval quality** and an **interval number**.

Interval numbers describe how many staff positions an interval encompasses. Seconds encompass two staff positions, thirds encompass three staff positions, and so on. The interval number relates only to staff positions; it has no direct relationship to clef or accidentals associated with the notes. The terms used to describe interval numbers are shown in Figure 7–1. The numbers are generally written as 1, 2, 3, and so on, but are read as unison, second, third, and so on.

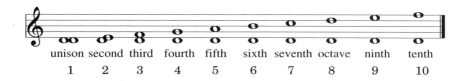

Figure 7–1

Simple intervals are those that are one octave or smaller, and **compound intervals** are greater than an octave. Except for the labels 9, 11, and 13 in popular sheet music, you will rarely encounter compound interval names. For example, a "twelfth" is more often called an "octave and a fifth." *Explorations* software does not use compound interval labels in its analysis. Intervals greater than one octave are described using their equivalent simple interval labels. Practice identifying interval numbers in Figure 7–2. Answers are given after the Summary at the end of this chapter.

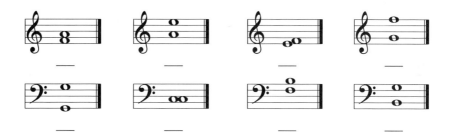

Figure 7–2

Interval quality is based on the size of the interval, that is, the number of half steps between the two notes. If two notes have the same name and encompass one staff position, the interval is called a **perfect unison**. Intervals between notes with the same note names that encompass eight staff positions are called **perfect octaves**. Study examples of these intervals in Figure 7–3.

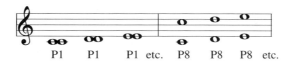

Figure 7–3

Chapter 2 discussed half steps and whole steps on the piano keyboard. These two intervals are generally notated as seconds on a staff. A **minor second** contains one half step; a **major second** contains one whole step (two half steps).

Intervals between members of major scales can be either half steps or whole steps. The chart in Figure 7–4 explains the intervals of seconds as they appear between notes in C major, that is, between notes without accidentals on adjacent staff positions. ("M2" means major second; "m2" means minor second.)

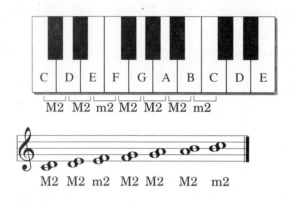

Figure 7–4

With the Screen Keyboard selected, click on middle C and click on the next white key, D. The keys darken to show the notes played, and the computer writes the analysis label below the staff: "major second." Click on the Up Arrow button and watch the notes move to D and E. The keyboard shows the keys used to play this major second. Another click on the Up Arrow button moves the notes to E and F. These two white keyboard keys have no black key between them and are therefore a minor second. View and hear all of the seconds on the staff by clicking the Up Arrow, Down Arrow, and Play buttons. Observe the keyboard keys that are used to perform these seconds. Learn to distinguish the difference in sound between major and minor seconds.

Practice labeling major and minor seconds in Figure 7–5. Write "M2" for major seconds and "m2" for minor seconds. Check your answers with those shown after the Summary at the end of this chapter.

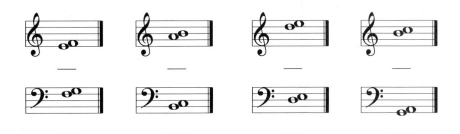

Figure 7–5

Because the number of half steps between adjacent scale degrees varies, the size of larger intervals between scale degrees will also vary. Figure 7–6 shows all thirds between notes of the C major scale. All thirds between major scale degrees are either minor (three half steps) or major (four half steps, or two whole steps).

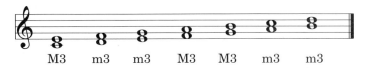

M3   m3   m3   M3   M3   m3   m3

Figure 7–6

Click on middle C and the E above it on the screen keyboard. This interval is displayed and analyzed. Click on the Up Arrow button and watch the notes move to D and F, a minor third. Count the half steps between the keyboard keys. View all of the thirds, their notation on the staff, the keys used to perform them, and their labels by clicking the Up Arrow and Down Arrow buttons. Listen to the difference in sound between minor and major thirds.

Figure 7–7 shows all fourths between notes of the C major scale. All fourths shown in this figure are **perfect** (five half steps), except for one **augmented** fourth (six half steps, or three whole steps) between F and B. Because there are three whole steps between these two notes, the augmented fourth is often called a **tritone** (three tones).

P4   P4   P4   A4   P4   P4   P4

Figure 7–7

As you continue through these interval discussions, play the notes in the figures on the keyboard and view their analyses. Listen to the intervals and learn to recognize their sounds. Use *Explorations* software to practice writing and recognizing different combinations of intervals. Select Practice from the Intervals menu, click on the New button, and design your own practice sessions and tests. For example, design a practice session that combines only major and minor thirds or only major and minor seconds. Combine these with larger intervals to form new drills.

All fifths in Figure 7–8 are **perfect fifths** (seven half steps), except for one **diminished fifth** (six half steps) between B and F. The diminished fifth, like an augmented fourth, has six half steps and is also called a tritone. Compare these intervals with the fourths found in Figure 7–7.

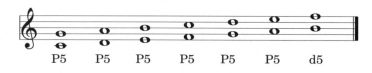

Figure 7–8

In Figure 7–9, three intervals are **minor sixths** (eight half steps) and four are **major sixths** (nine half steps). Compare these intervals with the thirds found in Figure 7–6.

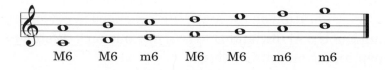

Figure 7–9

In Figure 7–10, all intervals are **minor sevenths** (ten half steps) except two: C to B and F to E. These two intervals are **major sevenths** (eleven half steps). Compare these intervals with the seconds found in Figure 7–4.

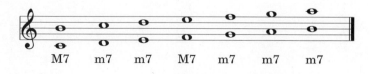

Figure 7–10

Memorize labels for intervals between notes of the C major scale and be able to recall them quickly. Intervallic recognition must be fast to be useful in playing and writing music. Challenge yourself to develop speed.

Because the pattern of half steps and whole steps is the same in every major scale, the intervals found in C major are also present in all major scales. To explore this, select Key Signature... from the Intervals menu, choose a key, and view the intervals found between its scale degrees, as you did in C major above.

The terms associated with interval quality (major, minor, perfect, diminished, augmented) may not be clear in your mind at this point. Practice and use this new vocabulary on a daily basis within the C major scale. Use *Explorations* software to explore, practice, and test these analysis skills. Develop the ability to recognize the sounds of these intervals as well. Chapter 8 discusses these relationships in more detail.

Summary

1. The distance between two notes is called an interval. Labels for intervals consist of an interval number and an interval quality.
2. Interval numbers refer to the number of staff positions encompassed by the interval. Interval qualities are determined by the number of half steps in the interval.
3. Simple intervals are those that are one octave or smaller. Compound intervals are greater than one octave.
4. Seconds, thirds, sixths, and sevenths between members of major scales can be major or minor.
5. Unisons, fourths, fifths, and octaves between members of major scales are generally perfect, except for one diminished fifth (B up to F in C major) and one augmented fourth (F up to B in C major). These two intervals are often called tritones.

Answers to Figure 7–2, Interval numbers, 1st row: 3, 5, 2, 7. 2nd row: 8, 1, 4, 6.
Answers to Figure 7–5, 1st row: m2, M2, M2, m2. 2nd row: M2, m2, M2, M2.

Music for Performance

Rhythms

Clap, tap, or sing the following exercises as a solo—that is, one person performing both parts at once—or as a duet—one person playing each part.

Melodies

Learn the following melodies. Observe the intervals present between scale degrees.

Canon: In the Evening

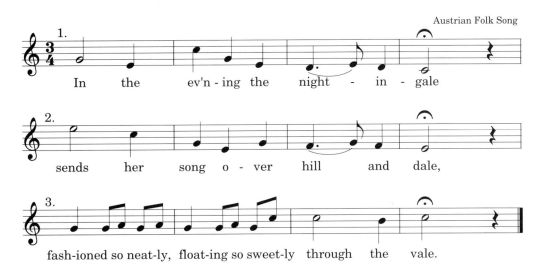

Austrian Folk Song

1. In the ev'n - ing the night - in - gale

2. sends her song o - ver hill and dale,

3. fash-ioned so neat-ly, float-ing so sweet-ly through the vale.

Shenandoah

American Folk Song

Oh, Shen-an-doah, I long to hear you, A - way, you rol-lin'

ri - ver, Oh, Shen-an-doah, I long to hear you, and a -

way, We're bound a - way, 'Cross the wide Mis - sour - i.

Swing Low, Sweet Chariot

D.C. al Fine means "da capo al fine," which, translated, instructs you to return to the top (the head) of the piece and perform until you reach the word *Fine*. Fine (pronounced fee-neh) means "the end."

Creative Exercises

Using the notes of the C major scale, write a musical composition for two violins consisting of harmonic thirds only. Choose whatever melodic intervals you like, but the two violins should always play a major or minor third apart. This may seem somewhat restrictive at first, but a great deal of variety can be created using interesting changes in melodic direction and provocative rhythm. Write out your composition using the *Explorations* Music Editor.

Practice and Tests

Do the written exercises in this textbook, and continue to explore the Intervals subject. Practice sessions and tests include intervals with accidentals, a topic covered in Chapter 8. Instructions for interval practice sessions and tests are given at the end of that chapter.

You may wish to try your hand at the exercises anyway. If so, read the instructions in Chapter 8, or simply figure out what to do based on your musical knowledge and previous experience with *Explorations* software.

Exercise 1: Analyze the intervals below. Write the appropriate interval label
beneath each interval, as shown in the first example.

____ P5 ____

Exercise 2: Analyze the intervals below. Write the appropriate interval label beneath each interval.

Exercise 3: Analyze the intervals below. Write the appropriate interval label beneath each interval. Draw dots on the keyboard keys used to play each interval, as shown in the first example.

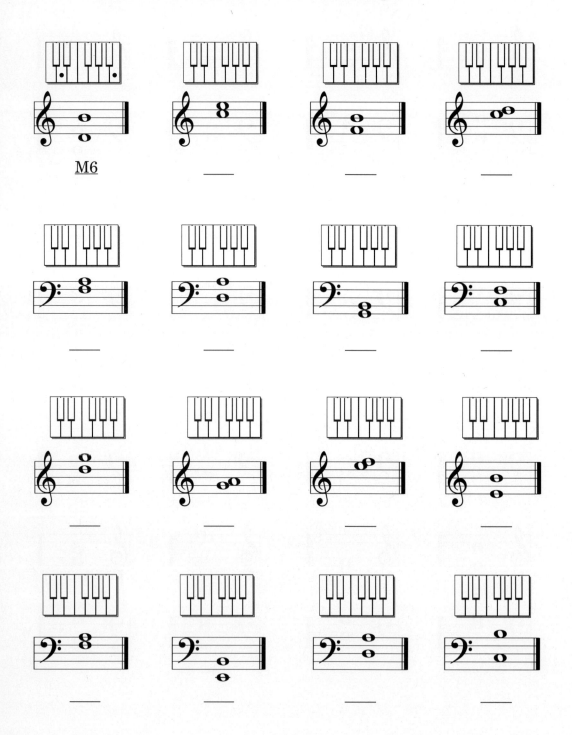

M6

Exercise 4: Analyze the intervals below. Write the appropriate interval label beneath each interval. Draw dots on the keyboard keys used to play each interval.

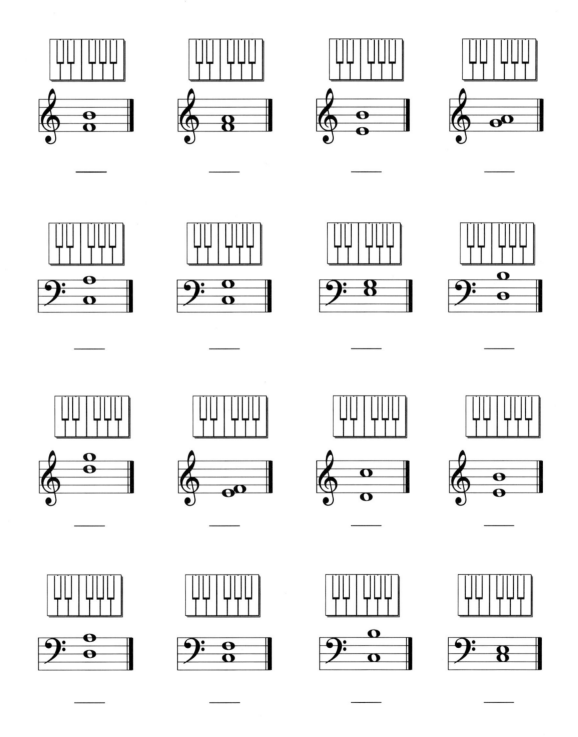

Exercise 5: Analyze the intervals below. Write the appropriate interval label beneath each interval. Draw dots on the keyboard keys used to play each interval. *Notice that the keyboard diagrams begin on a different pitch than do the diagrams in Exercise 4.*

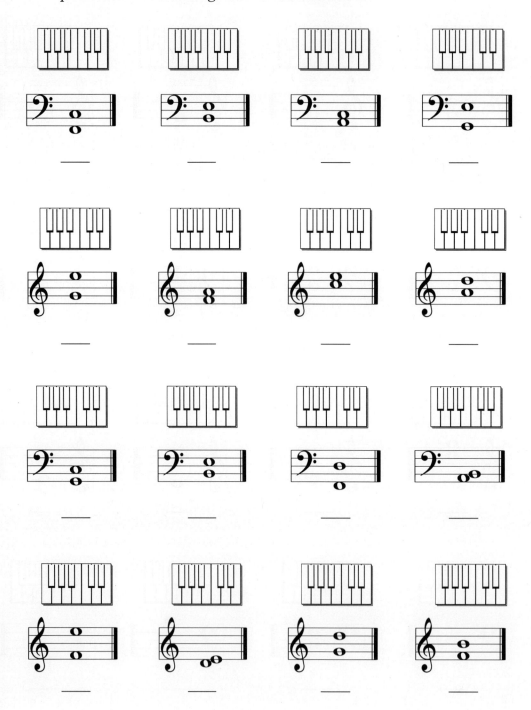

8 Intervals II

This chapter continues to use Intervals from the Subject menu for exploration. It will be helpful to select Screen Keyboard to view the piano keys associated with each interval. You may wish to use your own MIDI keyboard to enter notes. Select Set Key Signature… from the Intervals menu to review how intervals remain constant between scale degrees within major and minor key signatures. Review the procedures for using *Explorations* software found in Chapter 7 if necessary.

Recognizing Intervals

In Figure 8–1 the intervals from the tonic up to each major scale degree are shown. Notice that the quality of all intervals is either major (second, third, sixth, and seventh) or perfect (unison, fourth, fifth, and octave).

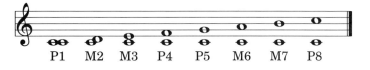

Figure 8–1

In Figure 8–2 the intervals from the tonic down to each major scale degree are given. These intervals are either minor (seventh, sixth, third, and second) or perfect (octave, fifth, fourth, and unison). Further discussion of this relationship is found in the section "Inversion of Intervals," later in this chapter.

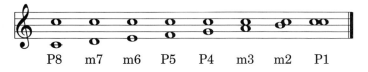

Figure 8–2

Intervals can be recognized by relationships within major and minor scales:
- Is the upper note found in the major scale of the lower note?
- If so, a second, third, sixth, or seventh is major, and a fourth or fifth is perfect.
- If not, is the lower note found in the major scale of the upper note?
- If so, a second, third, sixth, or seventh is minor, and a fourth or fifth is perfect.

Intervals and Accidentals

When composers use accidentals not found in the key signature, the qualities of intervals are changed. These intervals are either larger or smaller than the standard intervals between scale degrees.

All four intervals in Figure 8–3 are thirds because they encompass three staff positions. The first third is major, followed by three examples of alterations to the notes of that major third. The major third becomes a minor third when E is lowered one half step and when we add a sharp to the C. A diminished third occurs when both accidentals are added to the interval.

Figure 8–3

Figures 8–4 and 8–5 show how interval qualities change when accidentals are added or deleted and provide the terms used to describe those interval qualities. Notice that accidentals do not change interval *numbers*.

Terms for Unisons, Fourths, Fifths, and Octaves

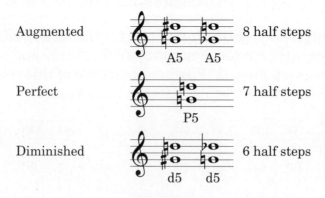

Figure 8–4

Terms for Seconds, Thirds, Sixths, and Sevenths

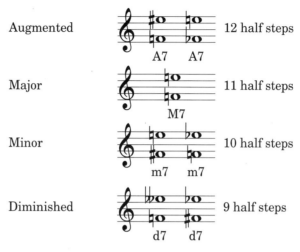

Augmented	12 half steps
Major	11 half steps
Minor	10 half steps
Diminished	9 half steps

Figure 8–5

A second approach to analyzing intervals starts with memorizing the intervals between the notes of C major (Chapter 7). To recognize intervals in other keys, calculate the interval without its accidentals, and then adjust the interval quality based on its accidentals. Be sure to listen to these changes in interval quality.

Start with the key signature of C major and review its intervals, viewing the screen keyboard at all times. Click on middle C and D on the screen keyboard to enter a major second. Add a sharp on the C to change this major second to a minor second. Click on the Up Arrow button to move the notes to a major second between D and E. Add an accidental to make this interval a half step smaller. Click once on the Up Arrow button again and add a flat to E, making the minor second between E and F into a major second. Add a sharp to the F to form an augmented second. Add accidentals to other intervals and view how their qualities change. Add both single and double accidentals to the notes. *Explorations* will give an analysis for each interval. It will also inform you if the resulting interval is rarely found in music or even if the interval is only hypothetical—that is, virtually never used by composers.

A third method for recognizing intervals is to determine the interval number by its staff positions and the interval quality by the space between keys of the keyboard. Learn to "feel" the size of major thirds, perfect fifths, and all other intervals. As you play intervals, learn to identify each interval's sound.

No matter which approach you use to recognize intervals, analysis should be practiced daily until it becomes automatic. Recognizing intervals helps musicians quickly recognize chords (discussed in Chapters 11 and 12) and also aids in playing or singing unfamiliar melodies (see Chapter 10).

Inversion of Intervals

You will have noticed in Chapter 7 that the notes used to form each seventh can be reordered to form a second. This is also true for the notes used in sixths and thirds as well as for fifths and fourths. This process, called **intervallic inversion**, is generally used only with simple interval labels. Intervals are inverted by lowering the upper note of the interval by one octave or by raising the lower note by one octave. This relationship between interval numbers is shown in Figure 8–6.

Unisons	become	Octaves	
Seconds	become	Sevenths	
Thirds	become	Sixths	
Fourths	become	Fifths	

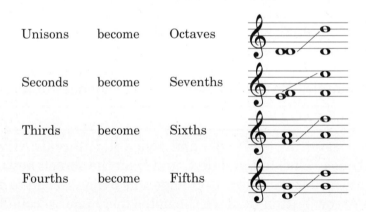

Figure 8–6

Notice that the interval number of an interval plus the interval number of its inversion always equals nine (9). The intervals in Figures 8–1 and 8–2 demonstrate inversion within the C major scale. Review those figures and observe the relationship between the quality of intervals and the quality of their inversions.

You can explore this process in the Intervals subject. Choose the Pointer Tool from the Music Toolbox and drag the lower note of any interval up one octave or drag the upper note down one octave. You can also play intervals and their inversions on the keyboard and double-check your accuracy by reading the computer's analysis.

Figure 8–7 shows the consistent relationships between qualities when intervals are inverted.

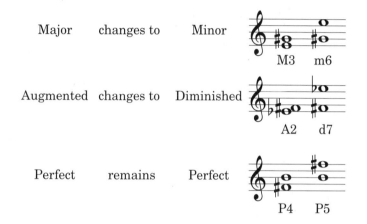

Major	changes to	Minor		M3	m6
Augmented	changes to	Diminished		A2	d7
Perfect	remains	Perfect		P4	P5

Figure 8–7

Figures 8–6 and 8–7 show these inversion relationships in only one direction. Inversions also work in reverse. For example, octaves, when inverted, become unisons (compare with Figure 8–6); minor intervals, when inverted, become major intervals (compare with Figure 8–7); and so on. When perfect intervals (unison, fourth, fifth, and octave) are inverted, they form other perfect intervals. Only perfect intervals have this capability.

Summary

1. Most intervals can be calculated by finding how the notes fit into each other's scales.
2. Interval quality is changed when an accidental is added to or deleted from either note but the interval number remains constant.

3. Intervals can also be recognized by calculating the interval between notes without their accidentals and adjusting their interval quality by reconsidering their accidentals.

4. Another way to calculate intervals is to memorize their size on the piano keyboard. Some musicians simply "feel" the size of an interval before applying the appropriate analytical label.

5. Depending on the specific number of half steps in the interval, unisons, fourths, fifths, and octaves can be called diminished, perfect, and augmented. Seconds, thirds, sixths, and sevenths can be diminished, major, minor, or augmented.

6. Doubly, triply, and quadruply augmented and diminished intervals are theoretically possible but are almost never used in musical compositions.

7. Simple intervals can be inverted by raising the lower note one octave or lowering the higher note one octave. Consistent relationships of inverted intervals are shown in Figures 8–6 and 8–7.

Music for Performance

Rhythms

Clap, tap, or sing the following exercises as a solo—that is, one person performing both parts at once—or as a duet—one person playing each part.

Melodies

Learn the following melodies. Observe the types of intervals used and how they are formed between scale degrees.

Canon: Meow, meow

Austrian Folk Song

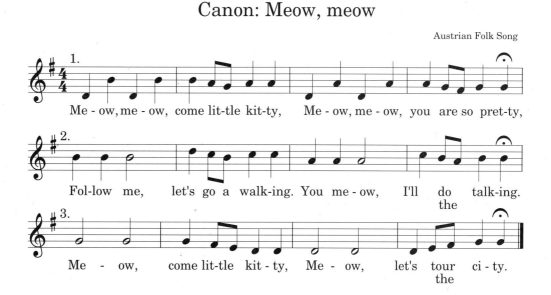

Roll Over

American Folk Song

Sing the first section nine times, then continue ...

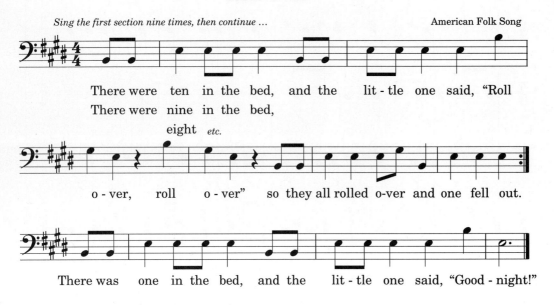

There were ten in the bed, and the lit - tle one said, "Roll
There were nine in the bed,
eight *etc.*

o - ver, roll o - ver" so they all rolled o-ver and one fell out.

There was one in the bed, and the lit - tle one said, "Good - night!"

All through the Night

Welsh Lullaby

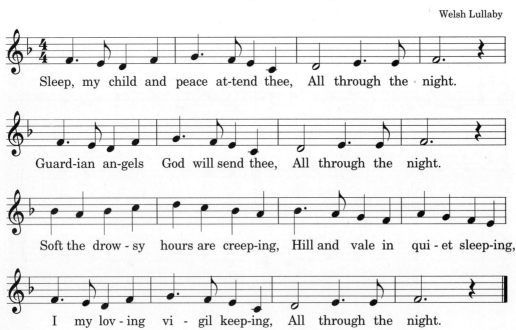

Sleep, my child and peace at-tend thee, All through the night.

Guard-ian an-gels God will send thee, All through the night.

Soft the drow - sy hours are creep-ing, Hill and vale in qui - et sleep-ing,

I my lov - ing vi - gil keep-ing, All through the night.

Creative Exercises

Choose a group of not more than three different intervals, and write a musical composition consisting of only those intervals. Do not restrict yourself to the notes of a major or minor scale; instead, choose interval qualities that remain constant and require accidentals. For example, you may wish to choose perfect fourths, perfect fifths, and perfect octaves. In such a case, you would not use any diminished or augmented fourths or fifths. You could also choose minor seconds, perfect fourths, and major sixths. Any combination will do, and each combination will give your composition a particular character. You might want to look through any of the six volumes of B. Bartok's *Mikrokosmos*. He often uses a limited number of intervals with a wide variety of compositional techniques.

Practice and Tests

Write Music   starts out with a single note. You are asked to write a second note above or below the first note, using a whole note from the Music Toolbox. In Ear Training, an interval is played with one note of the interval given on the staff. Be sure to add all necessary accidentals to notate the interval accurately. When you are done, click the Ready button.

Analyze Music   presents a written interval or, in Ear Training, the example is played. Your task is to enter the proper analysis label using the Entry Window. After you have entered an interval quality and an interval number, click the Enter button.

Keyboard   opens the Screen Keyboard for this type of activity, but you may use your MIDI instrument if you wish. A key is gray on the Screen Keyboard. You are asked to click on the second key of an interval, above or below the given key. In Ear Training drills, you see the gray key and hear an interval played. Click on the key of the other note in the interval.

Exercise 1: Analyze the intervals below. Write the appropriate interval label
beneath each interval, as shown in the first example.

Exercise 2: Analyze the intervals below. Write the appropriate interval label beneath each interval. Draw dots on the keyboard keys used to play each interval, as shown in the first example.

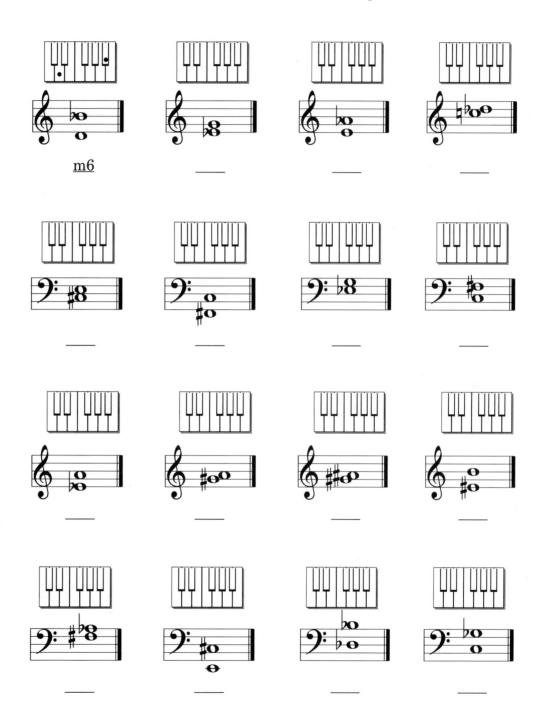

m6

Exercise 3: Analyze the intervals below. Write the appropriate interval label beneath each interval. Draw dots on the keyboard keys used to play each interval.

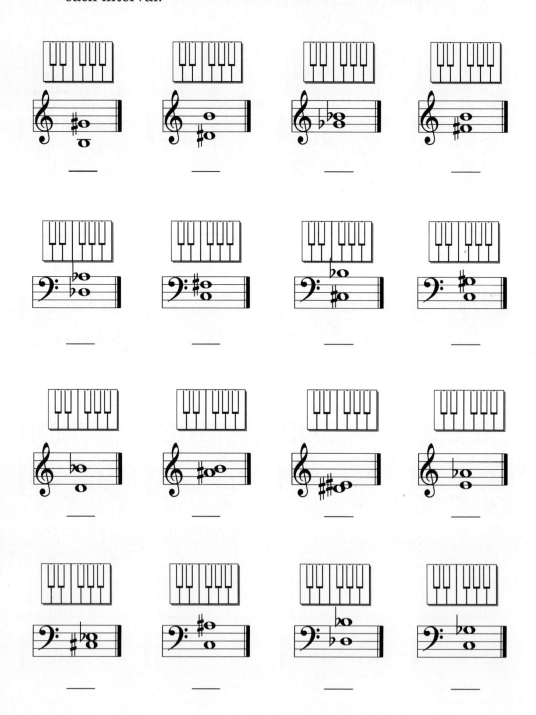

Exercise 4: Analyze the intervals below. Write the appropriate interval label beneath each interval. Draw dots on the keyboard keys used to play each interval. *Notice that the keyboard diagrams begin on a different pitch than do the diagrams in Exercises 2 and 3.*

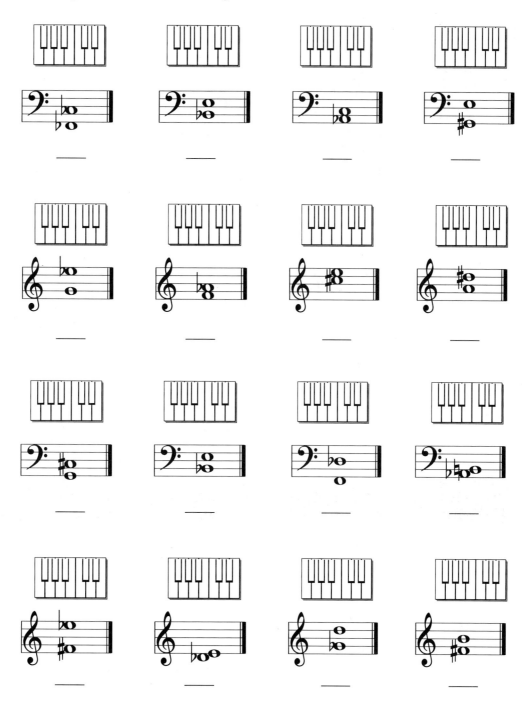

9 *Compound and Asymmetrical Meter*

Chapter 3 discussed simple meter. This chapter will continue to use the Rhythm subject as shown at the beginning of Chapter 3. If necessary, review those methods for using the Rhythm subject in *Explorations* software.

Compound Meter

Just as each measure is divided into beats, beats are further divided into subdivisions. Time signatures for simple meter imply that each beat will be subdivided normally into two parts. This is the feeling one gets from polkas or rock music. Compound- meter time signatures imply that each beat will be subdivided into three parts. Nineteenth-century hunting songs and barcaroles are generally written in compound meter. Music from the Swing Era also gives the "rolling" feeling of compound meter.

Compound meter is most often represented by the time signatures in Figure 9–1.

$$\frac{6}{8} \qquad \frac{9}{8} \qquad \frac{12}{8}$$

Figure 9–1

Within the Rhythm subject, select Set Time Signature... from the Rhythm menu. Enter each time signature shown in Figure 9–1 and view it with its subdivisions. Notice that *Explorations* software notates the beat with a dotted quarter note, subdividing the beat into three eighth notes. These are the most commonly used note values for subdivision in compound meter.

The differences between simple and compound time signatures are outlined in Figure 9–2. These conditions occur when musical compositions have moderate tempos and standard notation practices are used. However, notation is not completely standardized and, as your exploration with tempo and beat in Chapter 3 revealed, the beat is not always represented by the lower number of the time signature.

At moderate tempos:

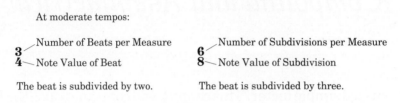

Figure 9–2

In the Rhythm subject, explore the compound meters and tempos listed in Figure 9–3. Which note gets the beat in each example? When you attend concerts, notice when the feeling of compound meter is present. Notice which styles tend to use simple meters and which styles use primarily compound meters. Experiment more with the combinations of tempo and compound meter within the Rhythm subject.

$$\frac{6}{8} \quad \eighthnote = 60 \qquad \frac{9}{8} \quad \eighthnote = 180$$

$$\frac{6}{8} \quad \dottedquarter = 90 \qquad \frac{12}{8} \quad \dottedquarter = 40$$

Figure 9–3

Asymmetrical Meter

Asymmetrical meters commonly contain five or seven beats per measure (see Figure 9–4). The most common time signatures for these meters are 5/4 and 7/4. Each measure is divided into groups of two and three beats. The first beat of each measure is always stressed, and the beginning of each new group of beats has a secondary accent. 5/4 meter divides its beats into one group of two and one group of three beats (two + three) or vice versa (three + two). 7/4 meter organizes its beats into two groups of two and one group of three beats in any order.

Open Tchaikovsky 6th from the Scores folder and click the Play button. Quintuple meter is an asymmetrical meter and is like having a duple meter group plus a triple meter group in each measure. Notice in Figure 9–4 that these two groups can occur in either order. In Tchaikovsky 6th (his sixth symphony, second movement), a natural accent on the first beat is followed by a weak beat. On beat 3 a strong beat occurs that is not quite as strong as the first beat, followed by two weak beats. Musicians refer to this type of 5/4 time as "two plus three." For an example of "three plus two," find a score to Dave Brubeck's "Take Five" at a library or music store.

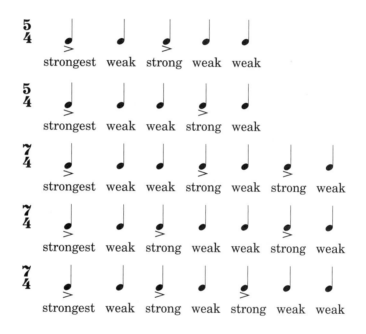

Figure 9–4

Special Rhythm Terms

Syncopation is the shift of accent to a portion of a beat or measure that is not normally accented. Syncopated rhythms place notes where no accent is expected and do not place notes where accents are expected.

The melody for an old barbershop tune is shown in Figure 9–5. It is found in the Scores folder under the name "Syncopation." Open it and click the Play button to hear it.

Joe Howard: Hello, Ma Baby

Figure 9–5

Select Rhythm from the Subject menu. The subject opens with 2/4 time. Click the Play button to hear the normal quarter-note beats. Select all quarter notes on the Rhythm staff by dragging the mouse over them and click on the Divide By Two button. Select the middle two eighth notes in the first measure and click on the Combine button. Notice how this syncopated rhythm contrasts with continuous eighth notes.

Hemiola, a Greek word referring to the ratio 3:2, is a rhythmic device used in 6/8 time where the metric accent of the bar is relocated. Instead of being divided into two groups of three eighth notes, measures with hemiola are divided into three pairs of eighth notes. "America" from Leonard Bernstein's *West Side Story* uses this rhythmic technique, alternating divisions of two and three eighth notes every other measure. When hemiola occurs in 3/4 time, the result is a rhythmic accent every two beats rather than every three beats.

An example of hemiola in 3/4 time is found in the Scores folder on the *Explorations* software disk. Open and play the score called "Hemiola," shown in Figure 9–6.

A. Corelli: Sonata in D Minor for Violin and Continuo, Opus 5, No. 7

Figure 9–6

Under normal circumstances, notes in simple meter are subdivided into two parts. At times, however, composers may wish to divide a note into three parts. These notes are called **triplets**. This notational method, shown in Figure 9–7, is used to divide undotted notes in simple meter into three equal parts.

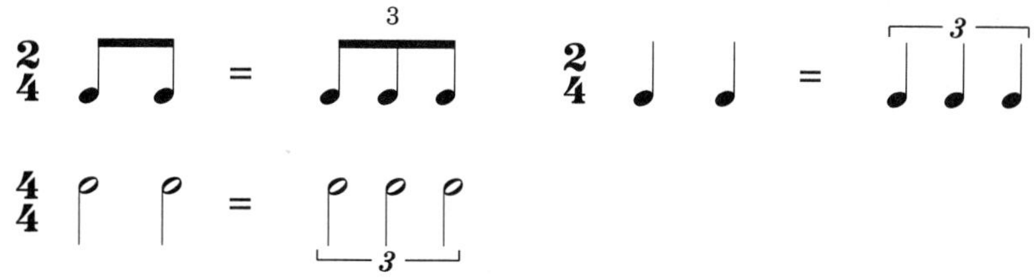

Figure 9–7

Swing is a method of playing music written in simple meter to make it sound as if it was written in compound meter. This method of performing the music causes the sound to be different from the notation that represents it. Figure 9–8 shows music the way it is written, and Figure 9–9 shows the way it is played.

> These two scores are found in the Scores folder on your *Explorations* disk under the titles "No Swing" and "Swing." Open these scores and play them one after the other to contrast them.

Figure 9–8

Figure 9–9

Select Set Time Signature... from the Rhythm menu. Enter 2/4 time and click OK. Select the first quarter note and click on the Divide by Two button. This demonstrates the normal subdivision of quarter notes into two eighth notes in simple meter. Now select the quarter note on the second beat and click on the Divide By Three button. This quarter note is divided into three triplets.

In compound meter, dotted notes most often get the beat. These beats are generally subdivided into three equal parts. The most frequently used compound meters have a dotted-quarter-note beat, subdivided into three eighth notes. From time to time composers wish to subdivide these beats into two equal parts. These values are called **duplets** and are notated in various ways, as shown in Figure 9–10. All four of these notational methods are used by major composers. Music notation is far from standardized in many areas. *Explorations* software writes duplets using the first of these methods.

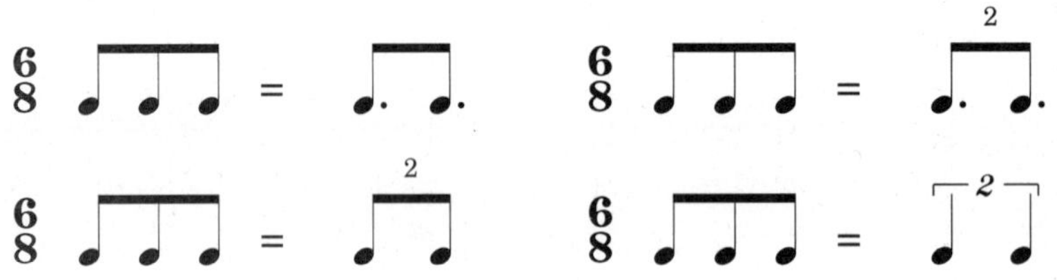

Figure 9–10

Select Set Time Signature... from the Rhythm menu. Enter 6/8 time and click OK. Select the first dotted quarter note and click on the Divide By Three button. This demonstrates the normal subdivision of dotted quarter notes into three eighth notes in compound meter. Now select the dotted quarter note on the second beat and click on the Divide By Two button. This quarter note is divided into two dotted eighth notes, one of the methods used to notate duplets.

1. Time signatures for simple meters imply that divisions of the beat will always be duple.
2. Compound meters divide the beat into three parts.
3. The most common compound meters are 6/8, 9/8, and 12/8.
4. Asymmetrical meters divide each measure into unequal groups of two and three beats. These groups of beats can occur in any order, and that order can change within the same musical composition.
5. Composers use syncopation to contradict the natural accent of each measure. Syncopated rhythms place notes where no accent is expected and do not place notes where accents are expected.
6. Hemiola is used in 6/8 and 3/4 meter to relocate the accent. Instead of being divided normally into two groups of three eighth notes, each 6/8 measure is divided into three pairs of eighth notes. In 3/4 time the two measures of three quarter notes each are divided rhythmically into three pairs of quarter notes.
7. When a performer "swings" the rhythm, music notated in simple meter sounds as if it were notated in compound meter.
8. When the beat is subdivided into three parts in simple meter, the rhythmic symbols are called triplets.
9. Duplets subdivide the beat into two parts in compound meter.

Music for Performance

Rhythms

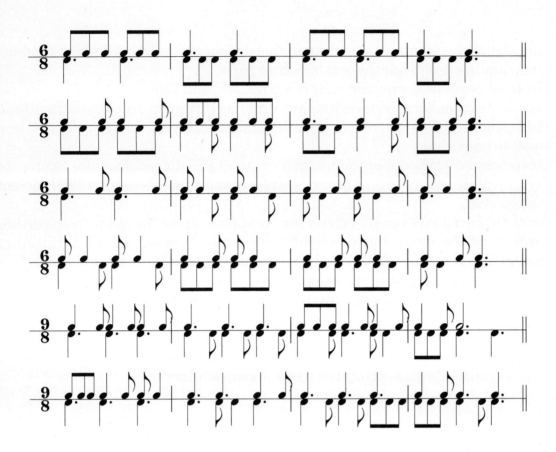

Melodies

Over the River and through the Woods

Traditional

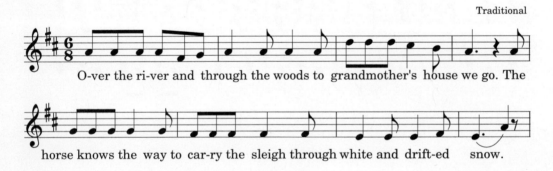

O-ver the ri-ver and through the woods to grandmother's house we go. The

horse knows the way to car-ry the sleigh through white and drift-ed snow.

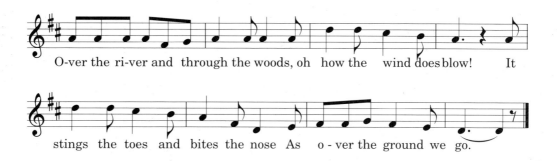

O-ver the ri-ver and through the woods, oh how the wind does blow! It stings the toes and bites the nose As o - ver the ground we go.

When Johnny Comes Marching Home Again

Patrick Gilmore

When John-ny comes march-ing home a-gain, Hur - rah! Hur - rah! We'll give him a heart - y wel-come then, Hur - rah! Hur - rah! The men will cheer and the boys will shout, the lad-ies they will all turn out, and we'll all be there when John-ny comes march-ing home.

Canon: We Ride through the Fields

Austrian Folk Song

We ride through the fields and the for - ests green, we know that no sport could be

great - er. If some-one should fall it won't mat-ter at all he'll just

pick him-self up and come lat - er. The com-pa-ny is just

fine, all care-ful to hold the reins light - ly. The

sun will al - ways shine, on ban - ners fly-ing so

bright - ly. Rid - ing on - ward on

hor - ses large and small. Rid - ing

home-ward and back in - to the stall.

Creative Exercises

Listen to at least one of the following compositions: G. F. Handel's *Water Music*, W. A. Mozart's *Duets for Two Horns* or one of his four horn concertos, and the third movement of A. Bruckner's *Symphony No. 4*. Pay close attention to the way these composers write for the horn (often called the French horn). Now try your hand at writing a musical composition for two horns in 6/8 time. Look in these musical scores and find the characteristic intervals that composers use when writing for horns. One such set of intervals is given in the music below.

Melodic intervals of seconds, thirds, and fourths with harmonic intervals of thirds, fifths, and sixths give music for horns a strong character. Remember, you are not expected to compete with the fine composers listed above. Talk to horn players and have them give you constructive criticism. Find a synthesizer with good horn sounds and preview your composition before presenting it to a horn player.

Practice and Tests

Practice sessions and tests for compound meter use the same two types of activities as the tests for simple meter in Chapter 3. Review the instructions at the end of that chapter if necessary.

Exercise 1: In each example below, add one note with a rhythmic value that will complete the measure. For example, in the first measure a dotted quarter note should be added.

Exercise 2: In each example below, add barlines that group the rhythmic values correctly according to the time signature.

10 *Diatonic Melody*

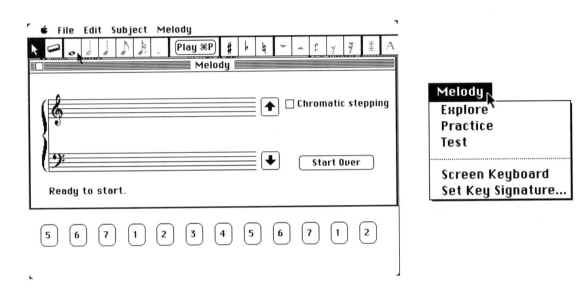

This subject opens with an empty staff and the remark "Ready to start" below it. Use the Scale Degree buttons at the bottom of the screen to play diatonic melodies. Listen to the sound and view each scale degree's notation. Each melody can be up to eight notes long. After hearing each note as you play it, click the Play button to hear the entire melody. The Arrow buttons normally transpose your melody to the next white key on the piano. When the Chromatic Stepping check box is checked, melodies are transposed by half step each time an arrow is clicked.

Add accidentals to any note in the scale using the Accidental Tools. This is useful when exploring melodies in the minor mode. The Scale Degree buttons in minor include all of its forms. Nondiatonic pitches receive a question mark (?) as analysis.

As you enter notes with the Screen Keyboard, the melody you play and each note's label appear on the screen. Select Set Key Signature... from the Melody menu to establish a new key; if the mode remains the same, the melody will be transposed to the new key.

A **melody** is a succession of pitches and durations that forms a recognizable, linear musical unit. The melody of a composition can occur in any instrument or voice but is found most often in the highest musical line. Secondary notes that are performed as a background to the melody are called the **accompaniment**.

Diatonic melodies are those that use only the tones of a major or minor scale. These melodies generally do not contain additional accidentals except for those found in the harmonic and melodic forms of minor scales.

Scale-Degree Labels

Musicians use **solfège** syllables and scale-degree numbers to label scale degrees of major and minor scales. The scale-degree chart in Figure 10–1 shows these for the keys of C major and C minor. These labels are used to sing melodies and to demonstrate melodic relationships between scale degrees. The solfège syllables are pronounced "doh," "ray," "mee," "fah," "soul," "lah," and "tee." The third, sixth, and seventh scale degrees of the natural minor are pronounced "may," "lay," and "tay," respectively.

Solfège	do	re	mi	fa	sol	la	ti	do
Scale Degree Numbers	1	2	3	4	5	6	7	8

Solfège	do	re	me	fa	sol	le	la	te	ti	do
Scale Degree Numbers	1	2	♭3	4	5	♭6	6	♭7	7	8

Figure 10–1

Notice how "do" is always the tonic in both the major and minor modes. Another solfège system exists that uses the tonic of the major mode as "do" and begins each relative minor scale on "la." This "la-based minor" is shown in Figure 10–2.

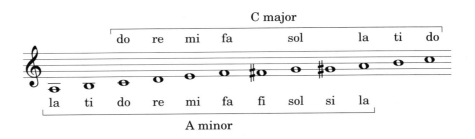

C major

| | do | re | mi | fa | | sol | | la | ti | do |

| la | ti | do | re | mi | fa | fi | sol | si | la |

A minor

Figure 10–2

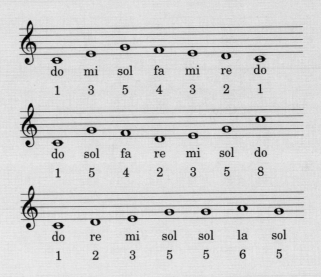

Select Melody from the Subject menu. This subject opens in the key of C major. Click on the Scale Degree buttons to enter the following melodies:

Listen carefully to the particular sound of each scale degree as you enter it. Then play each entire melody by clicking on the Play button. Click the Start Over button before entering each new melody. Click on the Arrow buttons to view and hear each melody in a variety of keys. The melody tones keep the same relationship to one another, except that the melody is higher or lower.

Select Set Key Signature… from the Melody menu and choose A minor as the new key. Notice that the buttons in the Entry Window change to include all necessary labels for the natural, harmonic, and melodic minor forms. Explore these scale degrees and listen to their characteristic sounds.

Scale-Degree Types

Each scale degree has a particular sound. Scale degrees can be roughly divided into two groups:

1. Stable scale degrees: 1, 3, and 5
2. Unstable scale degrees: 2, 4, 6, and 7

Figure 10–3 shows these two groups in the key of C major and in the key of C minor.

Figure 10–3

Select Open Score… from the File menu, and open "Beethoven Archduke Trio" from the Scores folder. Click on the Play button. You will notice that this melody sounds like a B-flat major scale. When listening to this melody, you may feel that the last note (A) wants to resolve to a B-flat that isn't present in the score. Beethoven actually wrote a B-flat at the end of this melodic segment, but leaving it out is probably the best demonstration of the melody's need to resolve to this tone. Add the final B-flat (dotted half note) in the last measure on the middle line of the staff.

Open the score "Incomplete Progression" and click on the Play button. Notice that scale degree 4 (F) does not resolve to 3 (E) as we feel it should. Add an E (half note) in the last measure on the lowest line of the treble staff and listen to this score again.

Unstable tones have a tendency to resolve to stable tones. This resolution causes the music to come to rest and creates a sense of completeness. Composers can establish tension in a melody by using many unstable scale degrees or by holding these tones for long rhythmic values before resolving them to stable tones. These resolutions depend on many complex issues in music and tend to occur along with changes in harmony. Harmony is discussed in the remaining chapters of this book.

Melodies combine stable and unstable scale degrees into common patterns. The remainder of this chapter will demonstrate only a few of the many possible melodic patterns and will show how similar patterns can appear in several melodies with different rhythmic features. Figure 10–4 contains a short "melody" that we often use in daily speech when we call out to someone.

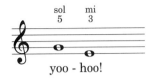

Figure 10–4

This call is translated into music as scale degrees 5 (sol) and 3 (mi) in the major mode, and it forms the basic interval for a common melodic children's "insult" found in Figure 10–5.

Figure 10–5

Figure 10–6 shows another melody that uses these same major scale degrees.

S. Foster: Camptown Races

Figure 10–6

Select Melody from the Subject menu once again. Click on the Scale Degree buttons in the Entry Window that correspond to the notes shown in Figures 10–4, 10–5, and 10–6. Click on the Play button to hear these melodies. Can you think of other melodies that use this pattern? Enter similar melodies by clicking on the Scale Degree buttons. Establish new key signatures, and play major and minor scales using the Scale Degree buttons in the Entry Window.

Figure 10–7 shows two melodies that start with the first three degrees of the major scale. Use the third staff to write a third melody that uses these scale degrees—for example, "Do, Re, Mi" from *The Sound of Music* by R. Rodgers and O. Hammerstein.

Traditional: Mary Had a Little Lamb

Traditional: Three Blind Mice

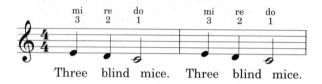

Figure 10–7

The melody in Figure 10–8 combines the fifth and sixth scale degrees with the first three scale degrees to form another traditional melody.

Traditional: Oh, Susanna

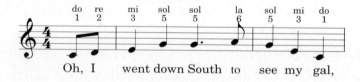

Figure 10–8

Figure 10–9 shows two melodies that begin only with stable tones. These stable tones make up the **triad** upon which the key is based. Triads will be discussed in remaining chapters. On the third staff, write a melody you know that uses these scale degrees.

Traditional: Skip to My Lou

Traditional: The Star-Spangled Banner

Figure 10–9

Melodies in the minor mode often use scale degrees 1, 3, and 5 as well. Two sample melodies are shown in Figure 10–10. In both of these melodies, the fourth scale degree plays an important role.

Traditional: Black Is the Color

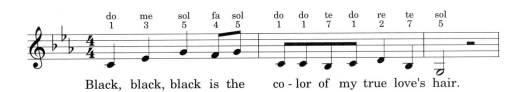

Traditional: Wayfaring Stranger

Figure 10–10

Enter the first eight notes of these and other melodies into the computer. You can enter them within the Melody subject by clicking on the Scale Degree buttons that correspond to the scale degrees printed above each melody. The Melody subject writes and plays these tones without their rhythm in order to emphasize the sound of each scale degree. Click on the Arrow buttons to view and hear each melody in various keys. Notice that the relative position and sound of each scale degree remain the same within each new key. If you prefer to hear the melodies with both rhythms and pitch, select New Score from the File menu and write the melodies using the *Explorations* Music Editor.

The melodies in this chapter demonstrate only a few of the many possible melodic figures in music. Learning to recognize the sound of each scale degree is an important musical skill that allows musicians to recognize the similarities between melodies and to notate melodies quickly in any key. As you listen to music, try to recognize which melodic figures are used in different tunes. Discovering similarities between various tunes increases your understanding of melody and enables you to appreciate more sophisticated melodies.

Summary

1. Solfège syllables and scale-degree numbers are used to label each scale degree.
2. Each scale degree has its own characteristic sound.
3. Some scale degrees are considered stable (1, 3, 5) because they give a sense of resolution. Unstable scale degrees (2, 4, 6, 7) resolve to stable scale degrees.
4. Many melodies share similar combinations of scale degrees.

Music for Performance

Rhythms

Clap, tap, or sing the following rhythmic patterns.

Melodies

Learn the following melodies.

Canon: The Cuckoo in the Forest

Music by Carl Gottlieb Hering

The Cuck-oo in the for - est, He sings his lit - tle song. He

cuck-oos to his sweet-heart, He cuck-oos all day long. The

folk in the vil - lage re - joice to hear him sing. They

know when they hear him that soon it will be Spring. Cuck-

oo, cuck - oo, cuck - oo, cuck - oo. Cuck-

oo, cuck - oo, cuck - oo, cuck - oo,

Canon: Welcome, April Sunshine

Austrian Folk Song

1. Wel-come A-pril sun-shine! Wak-en all the flow-ers.

2. Long we've wait-ed for your warm rays.

3. Winds come scat-ter the dark grey rain clouds.

4. Bring to us ma-ny bright and sun-ny days.

The Old Woman's Courtship

Appalachian Game Song

1. Old wo-man, old wo-man, are you fond of smok-ing?
2. Old wo-man, old wo-man, are you fond of card-ing?
3. Old wo-man, old wo-man, will you let me court you?
4. Old wo-man, old wo-man, don't you want to marry me?

1. Speak a lit-tle loud-er, Sir, I'm ra-ther hard of hear-ing!
2. Speak a lit-tle loud-er, Sir, I'm ra-ther hard of hear-ing!
3. Speak a lit-tle loud-er, Sir, I just be-gin to hear you!
4. Lord have mer-cy on my soul, I think that now I hear you!

Creative Exercises

Write several melodies based on your experience with *Explorations* software. In practice sessions and tests, described below, the computer actually composes melodies for your exercises. Imitate these melodies, exploring the use of stable and unstable tones. Use the notes of a major or one of the three forms of the minor mode. Which tones seem to desire resolution to which other tones? Write the final version of your melodies using the Music Editor.

Practice and Tests

Write Music   displays a single note with its analysis, along with a series of scale-degree labels. You are asked to write the remaining notes of the melody using a whole note from the Music Toolbox. In Ear Training, a single note is given and a melody is played. You are asked to notate that melody. As you write the notes, the analysis of those notes appears. If you wish to make changes along the way, drag the notes with the Pointer Tool. When you are finished, click the Ready button.

Analyze Music   presents a melody on the staff, or, in Ear Training, the example is played. Your task is to enter the proper scale-degree label using the Entry Window. You will notice that the Scale Degree buttons do not make sounds as they do in the Explore activity. This is good for you because it forces you to make those sounds in your own mind and not depend on the computer to help so much.

Keyboard   opens the Screen Keyboard for this type of activity, but you may use your MIDI instrument if you wish. The gray key on the Screen Keyboard corresponds to the first note of a melody on the staff. In ear-training drills, the computer plays the melody, displaying only the first note. Play each example on the keyboard. The Screen Keyboard will not make any sound. The goal is to hear these sounds in your head as you click the correct notes.

Exercise 1: Analyze the scale degrees within the major key signatures shown below. Write the appropriate scale-degree label beneath each note.

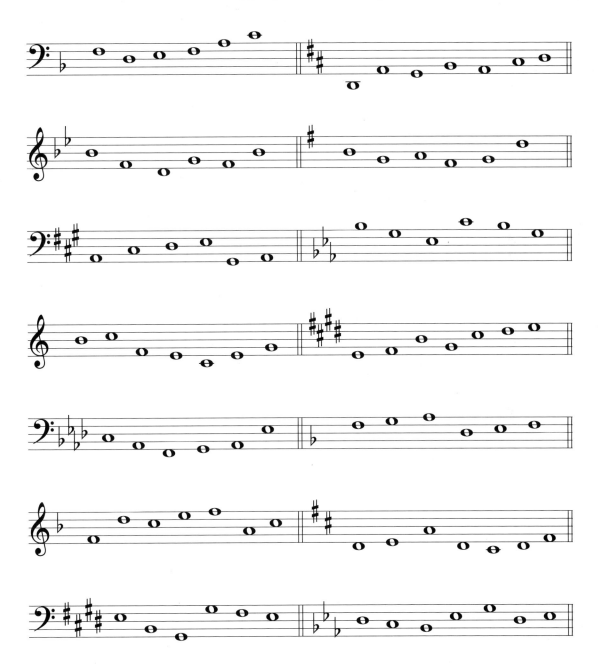

Exercise 2: Analyze the scale degrees within the minor key signatures shown below. Write the appropriate scale-degree label beneath each note.

11 *Triads*

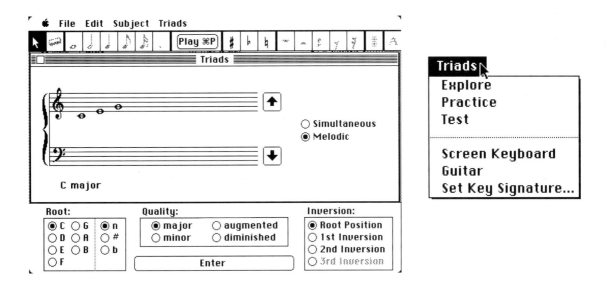

When you select this subject, three notes appear on a grand staff that form a C major triad. You may move any note by dragging it with the Pointer Tool from the Music Toolbox. You can also add accidentals with the Accidental Tools. Each time you alter a note, the triad's analysis is written below the staff.

You can establish a key signature by selecting Set Key Signature... item from the Triads menu. The Up Arrow and Down Arrow buttons in the Subject Window move all notes up or down by staff position within the key signature. This allows you to observe the qualities of triads within each scale.

The Simultaneous and Melodic radio buttons establish how the triads are played (by clicking the Play button) and displayed.

The Entry Window allows you to request a specific triad by choosing a root, a quality, and an inversion. The n, #, and b radio buttons represent natural, sharp, and flat. After your selections, click the Enter button to see and hear the triad.

Use the Screen Keyboard or your MIDI instrument to enter notes if you like. If the notes of the triad are played one at a time, the first note is displayed with its name. The second note is added to it, and their interval is analyzed below the staff. When the third note is played, the triad analysis is written. If the collection of tones does not form a triad, the message "Not a common triad" is written below the staff. If you play the notes simultaneously on a MIDI keyboard, the computer notates the entire triad and writes its analysis immediately. Selecting Guitar from the Triads menu allows you to enter triads using a graphic guitar fingerboard. See Appendix G for instructions.

Triads are three-note musical structures. The three members of a triad are called the **root**, the **third**, and the **fifth**. Two triads are shown in Figure 11–1.

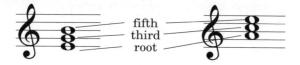

Figure 11–1

- The root is the note on which the triad is based.
- The third is a note located a third above the root.
- The fifth is a note located a fifth above the root.

Each triad has a particular quality based on the interval quality of its third and fifth. These qualities are shown in Figure 11–2. The labels beneath the triads are called **pop chord symbols**. They are a shorthand method for indicating chords in a composition. Major and minor triads are used most often in musical compositions; diminished triads are used fairly often, and augmented triads are quite rare.

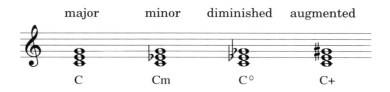

Figure 11–2

> Within the Triads subject, click on the Up Arrow and Down Arrow buttons to move the written triad to different staff positions. Choose Screen Keyboard from the Triads menu to see how these triads are played on keyboard instruments. Notice that all notes of each triad are located on lines or on spaces of a staff. When moving the written triad up and down the staff, notice that most triads are major or minor within any key signature. Only one diminished triad occurs in each key, based on the leading tone in major and the supertonic in minor. Additional accidentals are *always* required to create an augmented triad.

Figure 11–3 shows how these triad qualities are played on the keyboard. You can play each triad type by combining major thirds (four half steps) and minor thirds (three half steps) in the proper order above any keyboard key. Notice the quality of each fifth.

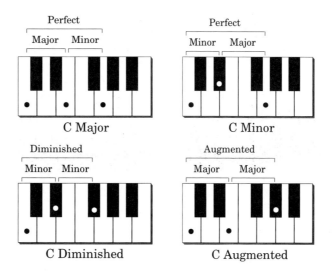

Figure 11–3

Play the triads in Figure 11–3 on the Screen Keyboard or on a MIDI instrument. Play triads based on other notes, and use the computer's analysis to check your work. Until you become fluent on the keyboard, you will need to count the number of half steps between chord members before you play each chord. With practice, finding the notes will become automatic.

Writing triads on a staff is simple if you follow some basic guidelines. Remember the names of the triad members: root, third, fifth. When a triad is written above its root, there is always a major or minor third between the triad's root and third and another major or minor third between the triad's third and fifth. There is always a diminished, perfect, or augmented fifth between the root and fifth of a triad. The *quality* of each third and fifth determines the quality of the triad.

Select Set Key Signature... from the Triads menu. Choose G major and view triads within that key by clicking on the Up Arrow and Down Arrow buttons. View triads within several key signatures. You will notice that no augmented triads occur naturally within any key signature.

Move the triad up the staff until a major triad occurs. Add a sharp to raise the fifth and form an augmented triad. Add various accidentals to other triads to see which new triad qualities are formed. When one of the four principal triad types is not formed, *Explorations* responds with "Not a common triad." If you move notes around on the staff, the computer may use such terms as "first inversion" and "second inversion" in its analysis. These terms are discussed later in this chapter.

Harmony

A triad is one type of **chord**. Chords are the basic building blocks of **harmony**. Harmony is the set of relationships that governs vertical organization of music. In a musical composition, notes of a triad can be written in any order and in any octave. The conventions, or "rules," of harmony determine how these notes are organized. Figure 11-4 contains examples of chords, all of which are based on the F major triad. Notice that the same triad members (root, third, and fifth) appear in different octaves.

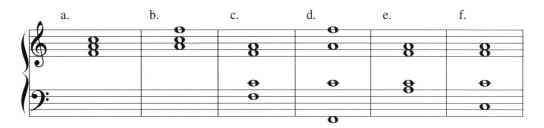

Figure 11–4

Some of the chords in Figure 11–4 have more than three notes, and one of the triad's three notes occurs more than once. This is called **doubling**. In Figure 11–4, c and d, the root is doubled. The root of a chord is doubled more often in tonal music than is the third or fifth. In Figure 11–4, e and f, the third and fifth, respectively, of each chord are doubled.

Chords are used in a variety of ways in musical compositions. Figure 11–5 shows a composition where each note belongs to a chord. The highest voice (soprano) sings a melody, and the other three voices (alto, tenor, bass) form chords under each melody note. The triads on which these chords are based are shown on the bottom staff of Figure 11–5.

Martin Luther: From Heaven Above

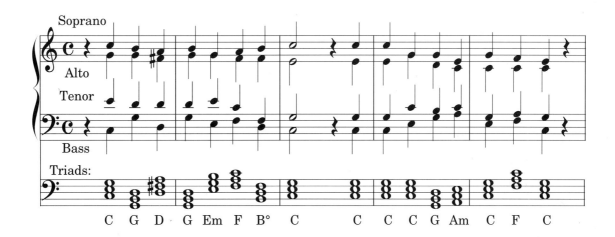

Figure 11–5

Inversions

The note that is present in the lowest voice is very important to the sound of a chord. In Figure 11–5 each chord has either the root or the third in the bass. The chords in Figure 11–4 have a variety of chord members present in the lowest voice. Figure 11–6 shows names given to chord **inversions**. Inversions are *always* named based on the lowest voice of the entire musical texture. To determine the root of an inverted chord, reorder the notes in thirds in your mind or on a written staff. The lowest note of that new ordering is the root of the chord. (See Appendix E for common analysis labels.)

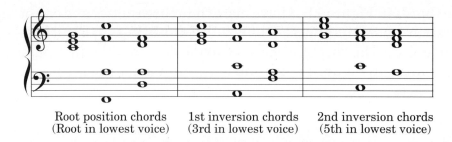

Root position chords   1st inversion chords   2nd inversion chords
(Root in lowest voice)   (3rd in lowest voice)   (5th in lowest voice)

Figure 11–6

Nonharmonic Tones

Figure 11–7 shows a keyboard composition that uses chords in the left hand to accompany thirds and sixths in the right hand. Notice that some of the notes on the treble staff are not members of the chord present on the bass staff. These notes are called **nonharmonic tones** or **nonchord tones**. Nonharmonic tones embellish the presence of a chord and add variety to the harmony and musical texture. Identify the chords in this example; they are the same as the vertical harmonies of the lower staff.

G. F. Handel: Suite in G minor, Passacaille

Figure 11–7

One of the most common uses of pop chord symbols is in writing **lead sheets**. A lead sheet consists of the melody of a popular tune and pop chord symbols to indicate the chords to be played with the melody. Each member of a performing group plays within these chords while one performer sings or plays the melody. Each member must know the notes of each chord to be played. The way each musician moves from chord to chord is called **voice leading**. Rules for successful voice leading will be discussed in Chapter 14. Figure 11–8 shows an example of a lead sheet and the triads represented by the pop chord symbols.

H. Carmichael: Heart and Soul

Figure 11–8

Learn to recognize, write, and play all qualities of triads. Use *Explorations* software to guide your study. Play triads on your Screen Keyboard or on a MIDI instrument and see the computer's analysis. Learn to recognize triad qualities visually and aurally using practice sessions in the Triad subject. Learning about harmony is very important for a strong understanding of musical structure.

Summary

1. Triads are the building blocks of harmony in musical compositions.
2. Each triad consists of a root, a third, and a fifth. The intervals between these chord members give each triad its particular quality. Major = M3 and P5 above the root, Minor = m3 and P5 above the root, Diminished = m3 and d5 above the root, and Augmented = M3 and A5 above the root.
3. Triads can be major, minor, diminished, or augmented. Major and minor triads are used most often in tonal music.
4. Pop chord symbols are used to describe the root and quality of a triad.

Music for Performance

Rhythms

Clap, tap, or sing the following exercises.

Melodies

Learn the following melodies.

Canon: C-O-F-F-E-E

Music by Carl Gottlieb Hering

C - O - F - F - E - E   Don't drink so   much   cof - fee!

It will   make you ve-ry ner-vous and dis-traught. You will ne-ver know just   what you've got.

Don't   be   a   sil - ly   clown!   It's   best   you   put   it   down.

Canon: Will Hans Arrive?

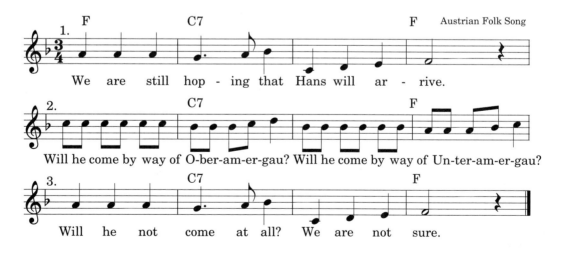

Austrian Folk Song

We   are   still   hop - ing that Hans will   ar - rive.

Will he come by way of O-ber-am-er-gau? Will he come by way of Un-ter-am-er-gau?

Will   he   not   come   at all?   We   are   not   sure.

The Whistling Gypsy

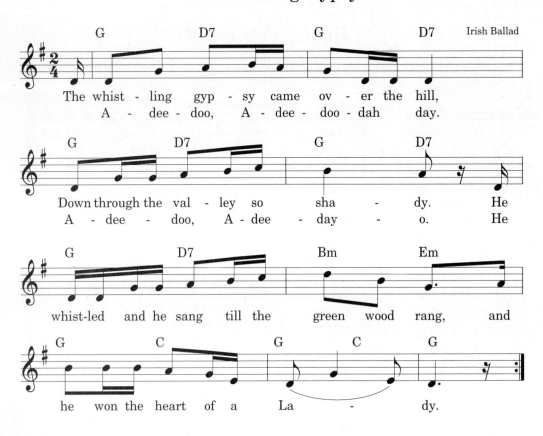

Irish Ballad

The whist - ling gyp - sy came ov - er the hill,
A - dee - doo, A - dee - doo - dah day.

Down through the val - ley so sha - dy. He
A - dee - doo, A - dee - day - o. He

whist-led and he sang till the green wood rang, and

he won the heart of a La - dy.

Creative Exercises

Write a composition for piano that uses triads in root position as its only musical structure. Those triads can be major, minor, diminished, or augmented. Contrast various qualities and play the triads in different parts of the piano keyboard. Repeat your chosen triads in rapid succession and experiment with interesting rhythms. Move freely between two or more different triads. Both Ravel and Stravinsky used C major and F# major in rapid alternation in musical compositions. Try out these and other triads.

Practice and Tests

Triad practice sessions and tests function in the same manner as interval drills discussed at the end of Chapter 8. The only difference is that you must add two notes to the given material in order to form a triad. Review those instructions in Chapter 8 if necessary.

Exercise 1: Starting with each piano key within one octave, play triads of each quality (major, minor, augmented, and diminished) on the *Explorations* Screen Keyboard or on a MIDI instrument. Use the Triads subject to check your answers and view proper chord spelling. Write these chord spellings on a piece of music paper or use the *Explorations* Music Editor to print them.

Exercise 2: Write the major scale for each of the following keys: C major, Eb major, F major, A major, B major. Build a triad on each scale degree, and label each triad using pop chord symbols. Write these chords on a piece of music paper or use the *Explorations* Music Editor to print them.

Exercise 3: Write the harmonic minor scale for each of the following keys: C minor, D minor, G minor, A minor, B minor. Build a triad on each scale degree. (Note: Use the minor seventh scale degree when writing a triad on the third scale degree. Use the leading tone for all other chords that contain the seventh scale degree.) Label each triad using pop chord symbols. Write these chords on a piece of music paper or use the *Explorations* Music Editor to print them.

Exercise 4: Write the triads specified by pop chord symbols below.

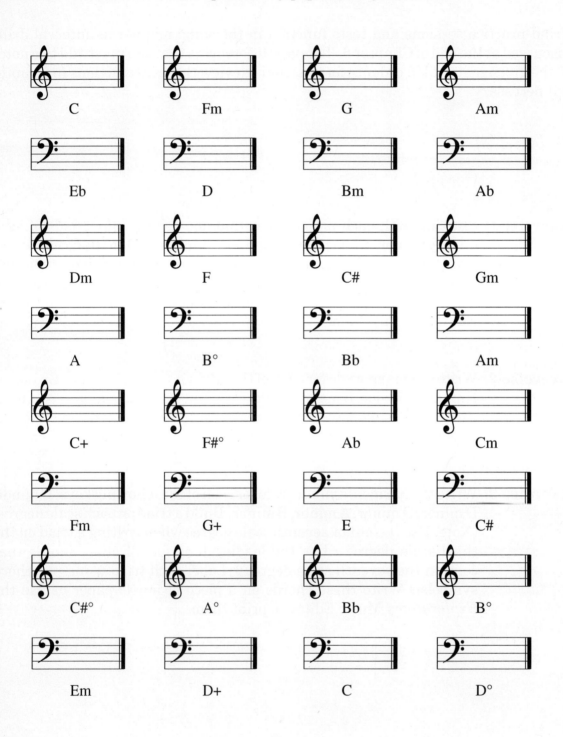

C   Fm   G   Am

Eb   D   Bm   Ab

Dm   F   C#   Gm

A   B°   Bb   Am

C+   F#°   Ab   Cm

Fm   G+   E   C#

C#°   A°   Bb   B°

Em   D+   C   D°

Exercise 5: Write the triads specified by pop chord symbols below.

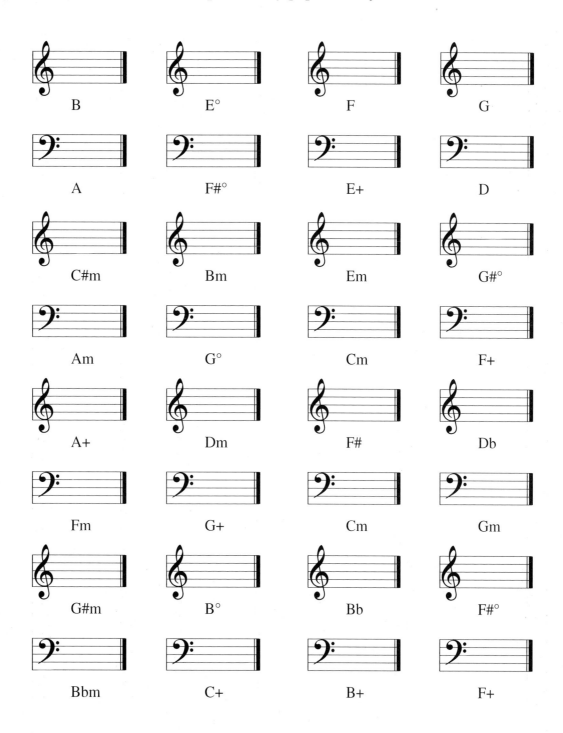

B   E°   F   G

A   F#°   E+   D

C#m   Bm   Em   G#°

Am   G°   Cm   F+

A+   Dm   F#   Db

Fm   G+   Cm   Gm

G#m   B°   Bb   F#°

Bbm   C+   B+   F+

Exercise 6: Write the triads specified by pop chord symbols below.

Ab

Bm

D

Eb

C

Fm

G

Am

G#m

Fm

C#

A+

C#m

Bm

Em

G#°

Fm

G+

E

C#

C+

F#°

Ab

Dm

C#°

A°

Bb

B°

Bbm

C°

Bb+

F+

Exercise 7: Analyze the triads below. Write the appropriate pop chord symbol beneath each triad.

Exercise 8: Analyze the triads below. Write the appropriate pop chord symbol beneath each triad.

12 *Seventh Chords*

Exploring seventh chords is possible by choosing Seventh Chords from the Subject menu. The interaction with *Explorations* software is exactly the same as that found in the Triads subject. The only difference is that the subject presents four-note groups that demonstrate the qualities of seventh chords. Review the explanation at the beginning of Chapter 11 if necessary.

A **seventh chord** is the combination of a triad and a seventh above a root. Like triads, seventh chords are part of the building blocks of harmony. The principal seventh chords used in tonal music are shown in Figure 12–1. Other combinations of triads and sevenths are possible, but those shown in Figure 12–1 are the most common. The tones of seventh chords are called the root, third, fifth, and seventh.

Figure 12–2 shows how these seventh chords are played on the piano keyboard. Learn to play these chord qualities on any note of the keyboard. Notice how triads and sevenths are combined.

> After selecting Seventh Chords from the Subject menu, select Screen Keyboard from the Seventh Chords menu. Move the seventh chord on the staff with the Arrow buttons and notice how each seventh chord type is played on the piano keyboard. Observe the quality of each seventh chord on each scale degree within each key signature.

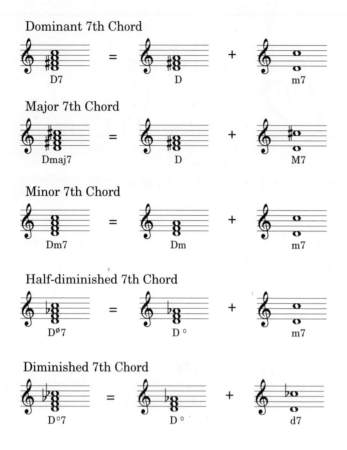

Figure 12–1

Major, minor, dominant, and half-diminished seventh chords appear naturally within all key signatures. To view a diminished seventh chord, select Set Key Signature... from the Seventh Chords menu and choose the key of G minor. Move the seventh chord on the screen to the chord on F. This F dominant seventh chord (F7) uses the tones of the natural minor scale. Add a sharp to the F to form the leading tone of G minor. Diminished seventh chords can be constructed based on the leading tone of any harmonic minor scale.

Inversions

Seventh chords can also be found in inversions, as shown in Figure 12–3. Like triads, inversions are determined by the chord member found in the lowest voice. (See Appendix E for more information on labels for chord inversions.)

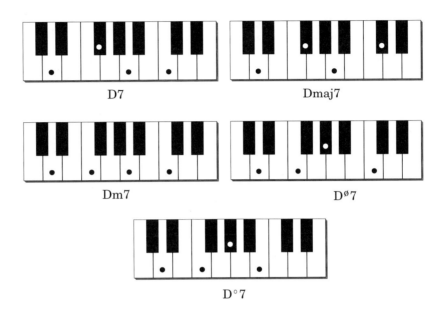

D7 Dmaj7

Dm7 Dᴓ7

D°7

Figure 12–2

Root Position 1st Inversion 2nd Inversion 3rd Inversion

Figure 12–3

Combining sevenths with triads gives more color to the chords of a musical composition. Seventh chords have been used by composers in virtually all periods of tonal music.

Select Open Score… from the File menu and open "Beethoven 1st Symphony" from the Scores folder. This example shows the use of several dominant seventh chords. Another score, "Grieg Suite," shows a series of seventh chords with a variety of qualities and inversions. Play and study these scores. Explore the use of seventh chords in modern popular sheet music and jazz classics available in any good music library.

Summary

1. Seventh chords, with triads, form the main building blocks of tonal harmony.
2. Each seventh chord consists of a triad and a seventh. The quality of the triad and the seventh gives each seventh chord its particular quality.
3. There are five commonly used seventh chord qualities. These seventh chords can be found in root position and three different inversions.
4. Pop chord symbols can be used to describe the root and quality of seventh chords.

Music for Performance

Rhythms

Clap, tap, or sing the following exercises.

Melodies

Learn the following melodies.

Sourwood Mountain

Kentucky Folk Song

Chick-en crow-in' on Sourwood Mountain, Hey de ding dang diddle-i day,
So many pret-ty girls I can't count 'em, Hey de ding dang diddle-i day.

My true love she lives in Let-cher Hey de ding dang did-dle-i day,
She won't come and I won't fetch her, Hey de ding dang did-dle-i day,

Canon: Dona Nobis Pacem

Sixteenth-Century European Canon

Dona nobis pacem is pronounced "do-nah no-bees pah-chem"
and means "grant us peace."

Comin' through the Rye

Words by Robert Burns

Scottish Folk Song

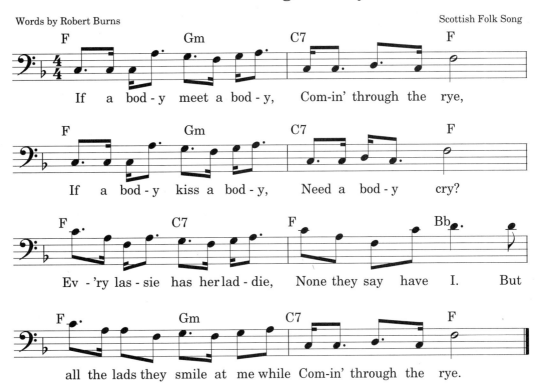

If a bod-y meet a bod-y, Com-in' through the rye,

If a bod-y kiss a bod-y, Need a bod-y cry?

Ev-'ry las-sie has her lad-die, None they say have I. But

all the lads they smile at me while Com-in' through the rye.

Creative Exercises

In the performance melodies for Chapters 11 and 12, pop chord symbols are used to indicate the triads and seventh chords used to harmonize those melodies. Play or sing each of those melodies, playing the chords with one hand on the piano. Don't worry about how to get from chord to chord (voice leading). Just get the chords "into your hands." Try playing these chords on a guitar. Explore the Guitar Window and Appendix G to learn how to play chords with proper fingerings.

After you have learned the progression for a song, write another melody that fits with the same chords. Use the notes of the chord to form an outline or structure, and use other notes to pass between those chord tones. Sing or play your new melody while someone else sings another melody that he or she wrote for that chord progression.

Practice and Tests

Seventh chord practice sessions and tests function in the same manner as interval drills discussed at the end of Chapter 8. The only difference is that you must add three notes to the given material in order to form a seventh chord. If necessary, review those instructions in Chapter 8.

Exercise 1: Write the seventh chords specified by pop chord symbols below.

Exercise 2: Write the seventh chords specified by pop chord symbols below.

Exercise 3: Analyze the seventh chords below. Write the appropriate pop chord symbol beneath each chord.

Exercise 4: Analyze the seventh chords below. Write the appropriate pop chord symbol beneath each chord.

13 *Chord Function*

When you select Chord Function from the Subject menu, three notes appear on a grand staff that form a C major triad. As will be explained, within the key of C major this tonic chord is labeled using the roman numeral "I." You can manipulate this triad in the same manner as in Chapter 11.

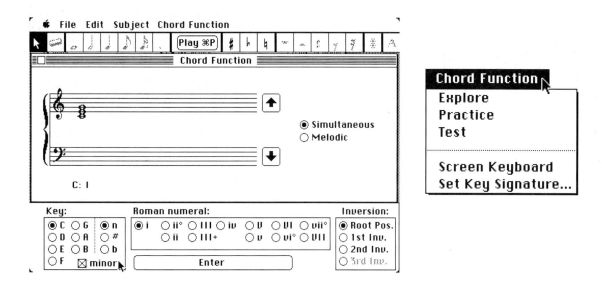

You can establish a key signature by selecting Set Key Signature... from the Chord Function menu. The Up Arrow and Down Arrow buttons in the Subject Window move all notes up or down by staff position within the key signature. This allows you to observe the qualities of each chord function within each key.

The Entry Window allows you to request a specific chord by choosing a key, a roman numeral function, and an inversion followed by the Enter button. The n, #, and b radio buttons represent natural, sharp, and flat. Clicking in the Minor check box establishes the proper roman numerals for the minor mode. To return to the major mode, click in the Minor check box again.

Use the Screen Keyboard or your MIDI instrument to enter notes if you like. If the notes of the triad are played one at a time, *Explorations* software responds exactly the same way as in the Triads subject. The roman numeral analysis is provided for all entered chords that are part of the chosen key. All others receive a question mark (?) in their analysis.

%

Chapters 11 and 12 discussed how to write and recognize triads and seventh chords. Pop chord symbols, introduced in those chapters, are labels that describe the root and the quality of a chord. Pop chord symbols are useful to describe *individual* chords. Other musical symbols show how chords relate to one another within a key.

Each scale degree in major and minor scales has its own particular sound (see Chapter 10). Scale degrees work together to establish the tonic as the key center. Similarly, each chord built on these scale degrees has its own particular sound and function in a key. Composers use these chord functions to establish keys. Figure 13–1 shows common triads built on scale degrees of the C major and C minor scales.

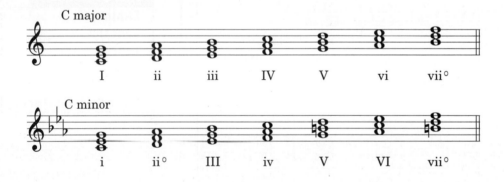

Figure 13–1

Musicians use **roman numerals** to identify chords on each scale degree. The roman numeral identifies the scale degree of the chord's root and the quality of the chord. Roman numerals show how chords are used to establish keys; they are especially useful in illustrating standard chord progressions, such as different types of blues changes, and in labeling cadence types.

Figure 13–2 shows the names given to each scale degree and the roman numerals most often associated with them. The minor mode uses two different chord qualities on several scale degrees, but the first of each pair is the most prevalent.

Scale Degree	Major	Minor
Tonic	I	i
Supertonic	ii	ii°, ii
Mediant	iii	III, III+
Subdominant	IV	iv, IV
Dominant	V	V, v
Submediant	vi	VI, vi°
Subtonic	not used	VII
Leading Tone	vii°	vii°

Figure 13–2

> Select Chord Function from the Subject menu. This subject opens in the key of C major and displays the tonic (I) chord. Click on the Up Arrow button to show the supertonic (ii) chord. Notice that this chord is minor. Continue through the chords of C major by clicking the Arrow buttons, and click on the Play button to hear them.

Cadences

Cadences are points in the music where certain rhythmic and harmonic ideas combine to give the music a sense of pause or completion of an idea. Each cadence consists of two chords and is identified by their functions. Figure 13–3 shows chord functions associated with each of the principal cadence types.

Authentic and **plagal cadences** are used in a musical composition wherever the composer wants to give a sense of finality. These cadence types end on the tonic chord (I or i), the key center. The authentic cadence is by far the most prevalent cadence type in tonal music.

Half cadences end on the dominant (V) and give the sense that the music is pausing on unstable ground and that there is more to come. Half cadences may be used anywhere except at the end of a piece.

The **deceptive cadence** ends on the submediant (vi or VI). This cadence is also called the interrupted cadence because in each case an authentic cadence is expected in the harmony. At that point, the composer substitutes a submediant chord for the expected tonic chord.

The two chords of a cadence are preceded by other chords that help prepare us for the arrival of the cadence. These other chords are variable, but some are used more often than others. Those used most often before authentic cadences are the IV (iv in minor) and the ii (ii° in minor). These are generally called the **predominants** or **dominant preparation chords**. At times the vi in the major mode is also used as a predominant.

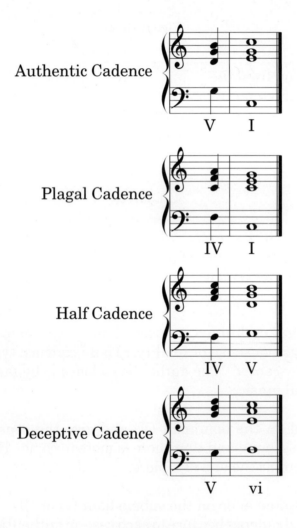

Figure 13–3

The *Explorations* disk includes a score in the Scores folder that illustrates these cadence types. This score is called "Cadences." Open this score and click the Play button to hear these cadences. Notice the music's sense of repose (or lack thereof) when each cadence takes place.

Summary

1. Pop chord symbols describe the root and quality of chords. Roman numerals also identify the scale degree on which a chord is built and show each chord's function in the key—that is, its relationship to other chords in the key. These relationships are indicated by roman numerals.
2. Cadences are points in music that provide a sense of pause or completion of an idea.
3. Particular chord functions are associated with each cadence type. Cadence types include authentic (V-I), plagal (IV-I), half (IV-V), and deceptive (V-vi).

Music for Performance

Rhythms

Clap, tap, or sing the following exercises.

Melodies

Learn the following melodies.

Canon: Shalom Chaverim

Israeli Traditional Song

1. Un - til we meet a - gain my friend, Sha-

2. lom, Sha - lom, Un - til we meet a -

3. gain my friend, Sha - lom, Sha - lom.

Canon: Bona Nox

Music by Wolfgang Amadeus Mozart

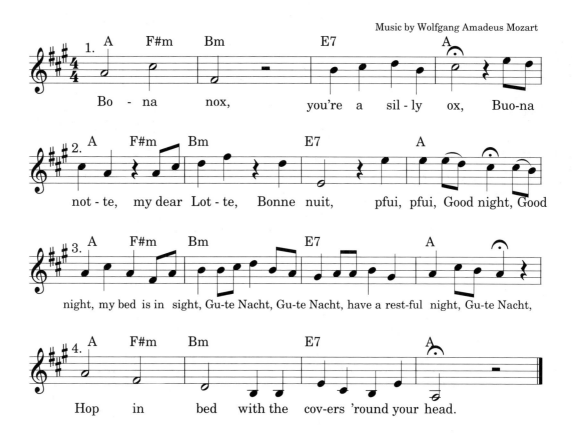

1. Bo - na nox, you're a sil - ly ox, Buo - na

2. not - te, my dear Lot - te, Bonne nuit, pfui, pfui, Good night, Good

3. night, my bed is in sight, Gu-te Nacht, Gu-te Nacht, have a rest-ful night, Gu-te Nacht,

4. Hop in bed with the cov-ers 'round your head.

Creative Exercises

Write, memorize, and learn to play the following groups of chords, represented by roman numerals, in the keys of C, F, and G major. Translate these labels into pop chord symbols for each key.

I IV V I
I ii V I
I vi ii V I

Learn the following chord groups in A, E, and D minor.

i iv V i
i ii° V i

After you can play these, write melodies that fit these chord progressions. Use chord members as the principal tones of your melody, and use other tones to pass between them.

Practice and Tests

Write Music displays a key signature and requests that you write the triad represented by a particular roman numeral. Use the whole note from the Music Toolbox to accomplish this task. In ear-training drills, a scale is played, followed by one of the chords of that key. Write the chord you heard played and click on the Ready button.

Analyze Music presents a key signature on the staff and shows a triad. The instructions tell you whether the key is major or minor. In ear-training drills, a scale and a tonic chord are played, followed by one of the chords of that key. Your task is to enter the proper analysis labels using the Entry Window. After you have entered a key and a roman numeral, click the Enter button.

Keyboard opens the Screen Keyboard for this type of activity, but you may use your MIDI instrument if you wish. The exercises are presented in the same manner as in the Write Music drills. Instead of writing the musical notation, you play the notes on the keyboard. As soon as the computer receives three notes, it evaluates your answer.

Exercise 1: Write the triad represented by the roman numeral in each given major key, as shown in the first example. Be sure to include any necessary accidentals in each chord.

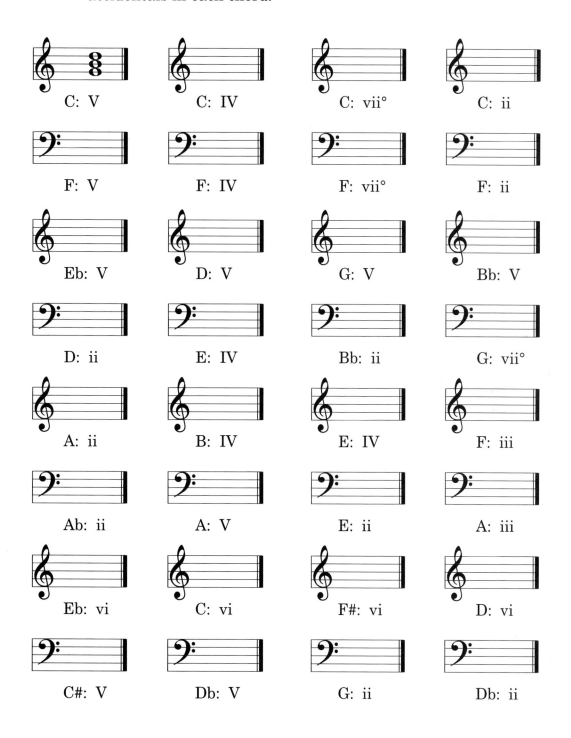

C: V   C: IV   C: vii°   C: ii

F: V   F: IV   F: vii°   F: ii

Eb: V   D: V   G: V   Bb: V

D: ii   E: IV   Bb: ii   G: vii°

A: ii   B: IV   E: IV   F: iii

Ab: ii   A: V   E: ii   A: iii

Eb: vi   C: vi   F#: vi   D: vi

C#: V   Db: V   G: ii   Db: ii

Exercise 2: Write the triad represented by the roman numeral in each given minor key, as shown in the first example. Be sure to include any necessary accidentals in each chord.

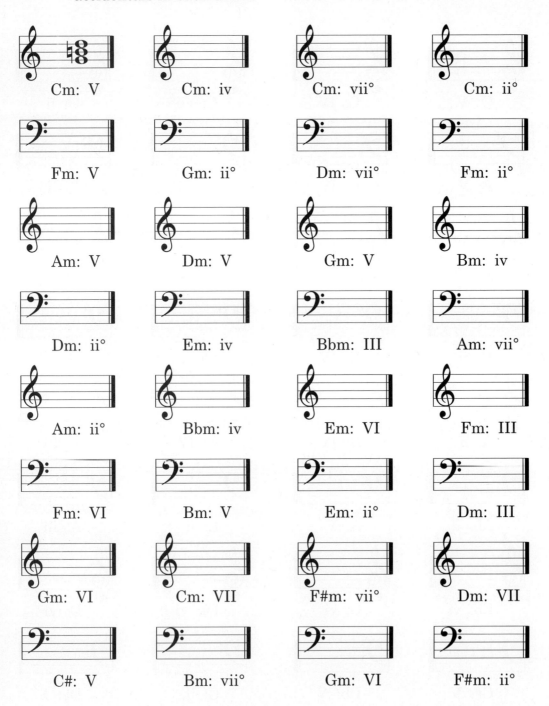

Cm: V	Cm: iv	Cm: vii°	Cm: ii°
Fm: V	Gm: ii°	Dm: vii°	Fm: ii°
Am: V	Dm: V	Gm: V	Bm: iv
Dm: ii°	Em: iv	Bbm: III	Am: vii°
Am: ii°	Bbm: iv	Em: VI	Fm: III
Fm: VI	Bm: V	Em: ii°	Dm: III
Gm: VI	Cm: VII	F#m: vii°	Dm: VII
C#: V	Bm: vii°	Gm: VI	F#m: ii°

Exercise 3: Analyze the following triads within each given major or minor key. Write the roman numeral that describes each chord's function within the key. For example, an A minor triad in C major would be labeled **vi**.

C: ___   Bb: ___   C: ___   Am: ___

F: ___   Em: ___   Cm: ___   Dm: ___

Bb: ___   C: ___   Gm: ___   A: ___

Cm: ___   Dm: ___   G: ___   Eb: ___

Em: ___   G#m: ___   Cm: ___   Em: ___

Ab: ___   D: ___   Bm: ___   A: ___

Db: ___   G: ___   Fm: ___   C: ___

Em: ___   Bb: ___   Em: ___   Cm: ___

Exercise 4: Analyze the chords found in the following musical examples. On the extra staff below, write the triad on which each chord is based, using whole notes to notate each triad. Don't be concerned that this puts too many beats in each measure; this staff is strictly for analysis purposes. Write each chord's pop chord symbol and roman numeral within the key. (See the first measure of each musical example.)

Scheidt

Eb
I

Bach

G
I

Exercise 5: Analyze the chords found in the following musical examples. On the extra staff below, write the triad on which each chord is based, using whole notes to notate each triad. Don't be concerned that this puts too many beats in each measure; this staff is strictly for analysis purposes. Write each chord's pop chord symbol and roman numeral within the key. (See the first measure of each musical example.)

Chopin

Eb
I

Schubert

D
I

14 *Voice Leading*

Recognizing and labeling chords is a useful way to get to know a musical composition. It is even more rewarding to be able to write your own music or to arrange an existing tune. This chapter demonstrates standard voice-leading models for moving from one chord to another.

We discovered in Chapters 11 and 12 that we can write the notes of triads and seventh chords in any order to form chords. An important term associated with chords is **voicing**. A chord's voicing is determined by the amount of space between its notes. There can be a great number of voicings for a particular chord because of all the different orderings of the notes and the varying distances between chord members that occur. Figure 14–1 shows some of the possible voicings of the C7 chord.

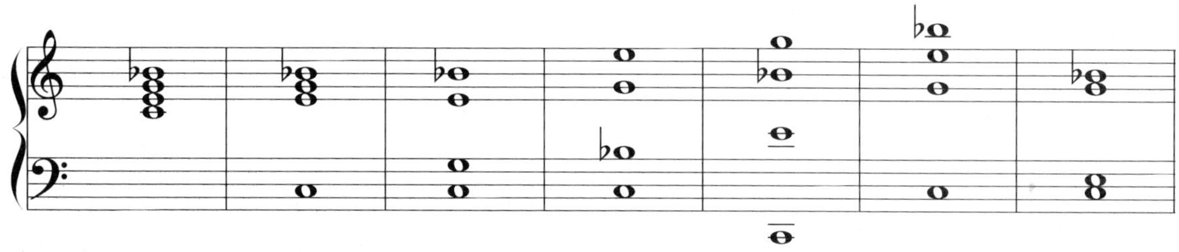

Figure 14–1

Explorations software includes a score in the Scores folder called "Voicings" that is identical to Figure 14–1. Open this score and listen to each chord. If you are playing the music on the Macintosh speaker, you may not be able to hear the bass clearly in all voicings. Playing this score on a MIDI instrument gives best results. Experiment with your own voicings of this chord. Choose another chord and write several voicings of it.

All examples in this chapter will demonstrate voice-leading principles using four voices (soprano, alto, tenor, and bass) in **keyboard style**. The three upper voices will be played with the right hand, while the left hand plays the bass. The distance between the soprano and the tenor should always be one octave or less. You will learn to write accompaniments to songs using the most common chord progressions.

Root Progressions

A **root progression** is a change of chord described by the interval between the *roots* of the two chords. The most common root progressions can be divided into three categories; all others are inversions of these (e.g., ascending fifth = descending fourth). Figure 14–2 contains an example of each of these types.

- Ascending and descending fourths (most frequently used)
- Ascending and descending thirds
- Ascending and descending seconds

Figure 14–2

Special attention is given to **common tones** in voice-leading models. Common tones are those notes shared by two chords. For example, the note C is not only part of C triads but also a member of the Am and F triads. A common tone between two adjacent chords is often held in the same voice as the progression between the two chords takes place.

Select Triads from the Subject menu. When the C major triad appears, choose the Pointer Tool from the Music Toolbox and drag the G to the second space A. Notice that the analysis now reads "A minor, 1st inversion." Since C and E were present in both triads, they are called common tones between the C major and the A minor triads. Now drag the E to the first space F on the staff. The analysis "F major, 2nd inversion" now appears. C and A remained constant and are the common tones between A minor and F major. Middle C was constant throughout these changes and is a common tone between C major, A minor, and F major. Experiment with other note changes and see which notes are common to other triads.

Ascending and Descending Fourth Progressions

There are two ways to write root progressions of fourths. The first method keeps a common tone in the same voice. This **common-tone model** is demonstrated in Figure 14–3. Ties show these common tones, but voices need not be tied to keep a common tone as the chord changes.

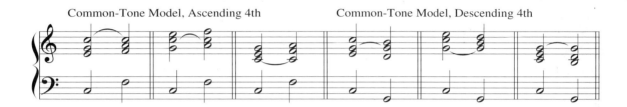

Figure 14–3

The second method for writing root progressions of a fourth is to move the voices without keeping a common tone in the same voice. Figure 14–4 shows this **noncommon-tone model**. Remember, a common tone between the two chords will always exist in the fourth root progression. However, in the noncommon-tone resolution model, no single voice performs that common tone in both chords.

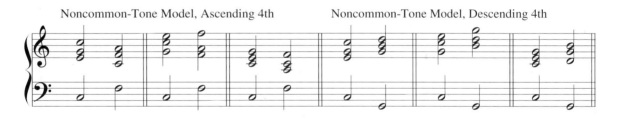

Figure 14–4

The strongest ascending fourth progression in tonal literature is the progression from the dominant (V) to the tonic (I or i). The dominant contains the leading tone, which requires special consideration in the voice leading. Notice that the second progression in Figure 14–4 is different from the others. When the leading tone is present in an *outer* voice, it generally resolves *up* to the tonic. In most cases, the common-tone resolution shown in Figure 14–3 is used. Notice that the example in Figure 14–4 has three roots and a third in the final chord. This root is **tripled**.

Ascending and Descending Third Progressions

Chords that are part of the same key and whose roots are a third apart share two common tones. When writing a third progression, keep these two common tones in the same voices (see Figure 14–5).

Figure 14–5

Ascending and Descending Second Progressions

The root progression of a major second is the most common second progression. When the root progression moves by major second and the bass performs the roots of both chords, all upper voices move in contrary motion to the bass voice. When the bass moves *up* a major second, all upper voices move *down* to the nearest chord members of the second chord. When the bass moves *down* a major second, all upper voices move *up* to the nearest chord members of the second chord. Models for this progression are shown in Figure 14–6.

Figure 14–6

Writing Chord Progressions

Figure 14–7 combines several root progressions to form a complete chord progression.

Similar progressions are used as a basis for accompanying popular and folk tunes. Play this example on a keyboard, or open "Basic Progression" from the Scores folder and click on the Play button. This example demonstrates many of the voice-leading models found in Figures 14–3 through 14–6.

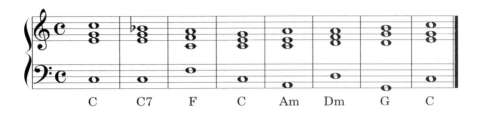

Figure 14–7

Composers use these models as a background to establish a consistent voice-leading musical structure. Most of the time this basic framework is embellished rhythmically and melodically. Composers add musical motives and embellishments to this structure to form a **musical texture** that creates the proper mood for a piece. The musical texture should interact well with the melody and should help express any text associated with it.

Let's use the chord progression in Figure 14–7 to explore some standard types of musical texture. After you explore these, you can develop your own. You are limited only by your imagination.

Iteration is the simplest method for creating a musical texture from a chord-progression model (see Figure 14–8).

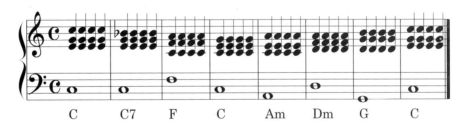

Figure 14–8

Another accompaniment texture is the so-called "**boom-chick**" style. Figure 14–9 uses this texture.

Figure 14–9

Figure 14–10 shows a more modern rhythm used within a "boom-chick" texture.

Figure 14–10

Figure 14–11 provides an example of **arpeggiation**, the presentation of chord tones one at a time. This device is sometimes called "broken chords."

Figure 14–11

Writing for Instruments

These voice-leading models and accompaniment types will get you started on a long learning adventure. As you begin to write arrangements for instruments, your most useful tools are your ears! Listen to how composers combine instrumental groups and how they build textures. Study scores to analyze their techniques.

When combining instrumental families (strings, woodwinds, brass, and percussion), write complete harmonies for the instruments within each family. Make each instrumental group sound effective alone, and the combined sound will be quite pleasing. When an instrument is used in the extreme ends of its range, it will generally stand out because of loudness or unusual tone color. This is appropriate only when it is truly desired, so use this technique wisely.

Take advantage of recent developments in computer software for writing musical scores and parts preparation. This can save a tremendous amount of time and make your music look great. Synthesizers can be used to double-check your score before you put the parts before human performers, or they can provide a practical alternative to live performance.

Writing for Choirs

The *Explorations* Music Editor allows you to write musical scores for keyboards and for choirs. This chapter has concentrated heavily on keyboard writing and its voice leading. Although voice leading for choral arranging is beyond the scope of this book, here are some exploratory activities to get you started.

> Select New Score from the File menu and click OK to write music with five grand staves. Now select Choral Style from the Compose menu. Notice that the letters S, A, T, and B appear on the left side of each grand staff. These refer to the soprano, alto, tenor, and bass voices of a choir. All soprano notes will be written on the upper staff with the stems up. All alto notes will be written on the upper staff with the stems down. Similarly, tenor notes are written on the lower staff with the stems up, and the bass is notated on the lower staff with stems down.
>
> The Soprano voice is chosen for the upper staff when Choral Style is selected. Turn to the score in Figure 11–5, and write the soprano line using the Note and Rest Tools. Click on the A and enter the alto line. Do the same for the tenor and bass parts. In order to select any notes, you must select the letter of the choral part. To see this, select all notes by dragging over them with the Pointer Tool. Notice that only the notes of the selected voices are outlined. This style of writing is useful in composing choral arrangements for church and community choruses. As your skill develops, you will want to purchase a more sophisticated editor than the one available in *Explorations* software.

Summary

1. Voicing is the particular arrangement of the tones of a chord.
2. A root progression is the interval between the roots of two adjacent chords.
3. There are standard voice-leading models available for each type of root progression.
4. Common tones are tones that are shared by two chords; for example, C is a member of the A minor chord and the F major chord.
5. Several root progressions can be combined into standard chord progressions. Many musical compositions may use the same basic chord progression. This is especially true in popular and jazz styles.
6. Voice-leading models can be used to write accompaniments for songs and as backgrounds for solo instruments.

7. Types of accompaniment textures include iteration, "boom-chick" figures, and arpeggiation.
8. Keyboard-style writing allows any number of voices to be written on any staff for the purposes of playing these notes on keyboard instruments. When voice-leading models are written in four voices, keyboard style places the upper three voices on the treble staff and the bass part on the bass staff. The upper three voices are played with the right hand while the bass is played with the left hand.
9. Choral-style writing places the soprano and alto voices on the treble staff and tenor and bass voices on the bass staff. Soprano and tenor parts are written with the stems up, while alto and bass parts are written with the stems down.

Music for Performance

Rhythms

Clap, tap, or sing the following exercises.

Melodies

Learn the following melodies.

Canon: Lo How a Rose E'er Blooming

Austrian Christmas Canon

Lo, how a Rose_____ e'er bloom - ing, From ten-der stem_____ hath sprung, From Jes-se's lin - eage com - - - - ing, As men of old_____ have sung.

Auld Lang Syne

Traditional Scottish Song

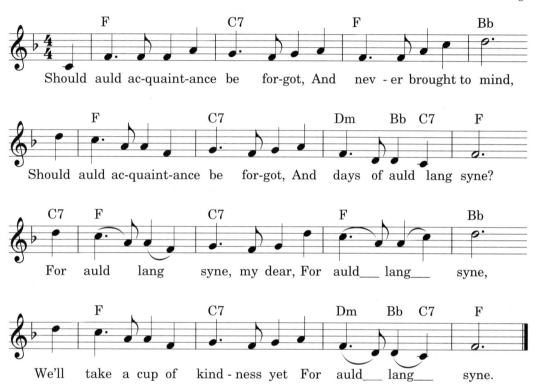

Creative Exercises

Write accompaniments for two songs found at the end of each chapter of this book. Many of the melodies have pop chord symbols that indicate their chord progressions. Find two melodies that contrast with one another, and experiment with different musical textures. Try to develop accompaniments that match the character of the melody and its text.

Exercise 1: Write the following chord progressions using the voice-leading models found in this chapter.

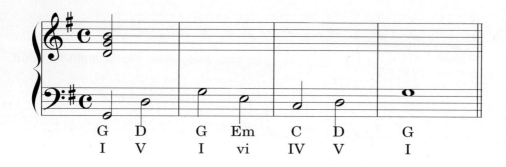

G   D   G   Em   C   D   G
I   V   I   vi   IV   V   I

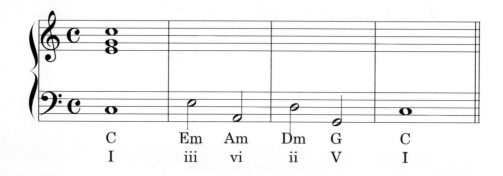

C   Em   Am   Dm   G   C
I   iii   vi   ii   V   I

Exercise 2: Write the following chord progressions using the voice-leading models found in this chapter.

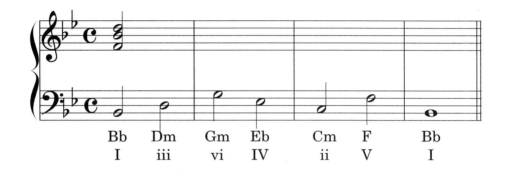

Bb	Dm	Gm	Eb	Cm	F	Bb
I	iii	vi	IV	ii	V	I

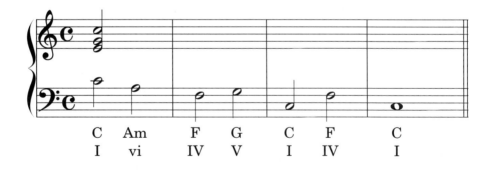

C	Am	F	G	C	F	C
I	vi	IV	V	I	IV	I

Exercise 3: Write the following chord progressions using the voice-leading models found in this chapter. When writing an example in the minor mode, use the harmonic minor—that is, add the necessary accidental to form the leading tone in each dominant chord (V).

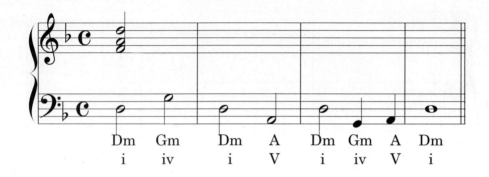

Dm Gm   Dm A   Dm Gm A Dm
i iv   i V   i iv V i

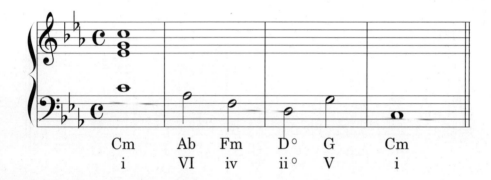

Cm Ab Fm D° G   Cm
i VI iv ii° V   i

Exercise 4: Write the following chord progressions using the voice-leading models found in this chapter. When writing an example in the minor mode, use the harmonic minor—that is, add the necessary accidental to form the leading tone in each dominant chord (V).

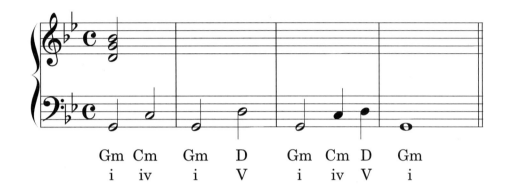

Gm	Cm	Gm	D	Gm	Cm	D	Gm
i	iv	i	V	i	iv	V	i

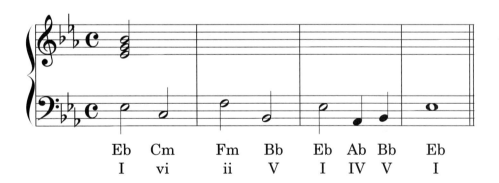

Eb	Cm	Fm	Bb	Eb	Ab	Bb	Eb
I	vi	ii	V	I	IV	V	I

A Macintosh Tutorial

This appendix uses *Explorations* software to teach you how to use the Macintosh computer. This discussion also introduces several aspects of *Explorations* software.

To start, turn on your computer. The switch is on the back of the Macintosh Plus and SE models and in the upper right corner of the Macintosh II keyboard.

For Macintosh computers with two floppy disk drives:
Insert a System Disk that came with your computer in the internal disk drive and insert your *Explorations* disk in the external drive. If you are working in a computer laboratory, use the System Disk provided by your lab personnel.

For Macintosh computers with a hard drive:
After the hard disk gets started (you will see a light flash on the hard drive), insert the *Explorations* disk into any floppy disk drive.

When the computer finishes its preliminary tasks, your Macintosh screen will look somewhat like Figure A–1. The area of the screen labeled "Explorations Disk" is the window for your disk. Other windows may also be present on the computer screen.

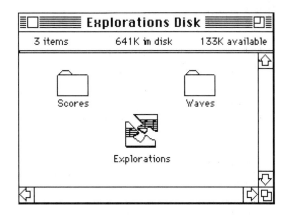

Figure A–1

Macintosh user manuals mention and define terms associated with Macintosh computers. The terms necessary to work with *Explorations* software will be discussed here, and you will explore these terms by using the software itself.

Icon **A picture that represents something.** An icon for each disk your computer is using appears in the upper right corner of the screen. The *Explorations* window contains three icons. The shape of the *Explorations* icon shows that it is an application, that is, a program that can produce documents. The other two icons are folders that contain *Explorations* documents.

Pointer **An arrow that can be moved on the screen by moving the mouse.** Move the mouse on a flat surface and watch the pointer move in the same directions.

Click **A quick push and immediate release of the mouse button.** Move the pointer into the *Explorations* window and position it over the icon labeled *Explorations*. Click the mouse button and watch the *Explorations* icon turn dark. Move the pointer to the Waveforms folder and click again. The *Explorations* icon turns light again and the Waveforms folder turns dark.

Double click **Two clicks in rapid succession.** Move the pointer to the Scores folder and double-click on that folder. If you don't succeed at first, try again. Try to keep the mouse stationary during both clicks. Notice that the folder opens and a new window appears labeled "Scores." This window has several icons in it, all of the same type. These are *Explorations* Score icons. You will use these musical scores as you read the material in this textbook.

Scroll bar **A shaded area on the right and bottom of a window that controls the portion of the material that can be seen in the window.** Click on the arrows of the scroll bar to move the items in the window a small distance. Click in the gray area to move the window a greater distance. *Explorations* also has other scroll bars that control loudness of sound or allow you to select note values to control the speed of the music. These scroll bars operate in the same fashion.

Dragging **Moving the pointer across the screen while holding down the mouse button.** Move the pointer to the word "File" in the upper left corner of the screen. Position the pointer over the word "File" and hold down the mouse button. A menu will appear, a group of choices that you use to tell the computer what you want it to do. Continue to hold the mouse button and drag the mouse straight down until Close turns dark. Release the mouse button. This choice closes the Scores folder that you opened earlier.

With these simple mouse techniques, you can explore and learn music fundamentals with *Explorations* software. Let's take a quick tour of *Explorations* and learn how to react to each type of symbol you will encounter.

To get started, double-click on the *Explorations* icon. The first time you use *Explorations,* the program will show you the "dialog" found in Figure A–2. A dialog is one way the computer asks for information from you.

The computer wants you to enter your name. Your name will be printed on all of your musical compositions and test results, so be sure to enter it correctly. Type your first name and press the Tab key. Then type your last name. Double-click on any name to retype it. When all is correct, click on the OK button. You only have to enter your name when you use the program the first time.

```
Welcome to Explorations!

Please enter your name as you
wish it to appear on your teacher's
grade list. Press the tab key to get
from one box to another.

First: [          ]

Last:  [          ]

              ( Quit )    ( OK )
```

Figure A–2

After you have clicked OK, the screen appears as shown in Figure A–3.

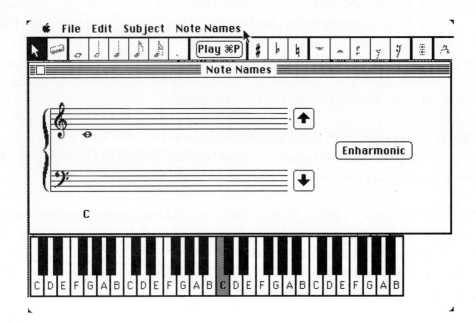

Figure A–3

Dialog	**A special window for collecting information from the computer user.** The window in which you entered your name was a dialog. You will use other dialogs later in this tutorial.
Menu bar	**The group of words at the top of the screen that indicate menus available for controlling the program.** You used the menu bar on the desktop earlier in this tutorial. You selected Close from the File menu to close the Scores folder.
Music Toolbox	**The group of music symbols that appear immediately below the menu bar.** You will use these symbols to write music notation on the staff in each Subject Window. The Play button allows you to play any music that appears in the Subject Window below it.
Subject Window	**The main window of the program that contains the subject you have chosen.** The Note Names subject appears when you use the program for the first time. After that, the subject you were using when you last quit will appear when you use the program again.
Entry Window	**The window at the bottom of the screen where guitar notation, music labels, or keyboard keys are used to**

	request information from the computer. Click on several keyboard keys, listen to their sounds, and watch the music notation change in the Subject Window.
Button	**A simple control of the computer that is activated by clicking it.** Click on the button labeled "Enharmonic." Notice that the music notation changes each time you click this button. The piano keyboard in the Entry Window is also a set of buttons.
Arrow buttons	**Special buttons designed for *Explorations* software. Clicking these moves notes up and down the staff in the Subject Window.** Explore these and see how the note moves on the staff. The piano keyboard also reacts to this movement.

To learn more about *Explorations* software, select MIDI Preferences... from the Edit menu. To do this move the pointer to the word "Edit" in the menu bar at the top of the screen. Drag the mouse (holding down the mouse button) straight down until MIDI Preferences... turns dark. Then release the mouse button. The MIDI Preferences dialog will appear on the screen as shown in Figure A–4.

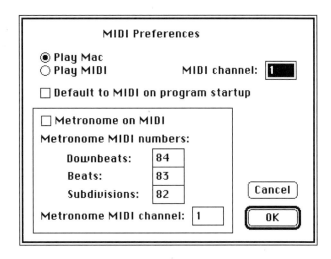

Figure A–4

Radio buttons	**Buttons in a group where only one of them can be selected at any one time.** Notice the two radio buttons labeled "Play Mac" and "Play MIDI." The Play Mac button is selected, indicated by the filled circle. Click in the circle for the Play MIDI button or anywhere on the words "Play MIDI." The Play MIDI button is now selected and the Play Mac button is not. The musical sound from *Explorations* software can be

played using the Macintosh speaker or a MIDI instrument. If you do not have a MIDI instrument, click the Play Mac radio button again to set the Macintosh speaker for playing music.

Check box   **A box in which an "X" appears when a particular item is selected. These boxes act like toggle switches. Click once to select the item and click again to deselect it.** If you own a MIDI instrument and wish to always have the MIDI played, click on the check box labeled "Default to MIDI on Program Startup." This way you won't have to select the Play MIDI button each time you use *Explorations* software. If your keyboard can be split, you may wish to use percussion instruments to play the metronome on your MIDI instrument. If so, click on the check box labeled "Metronome on MIDI." You can set the MIDI key number for the different parts of the metronome's ticks.

Text box   **A box where information is typed on the computer keyboard to control the program.** You encountered text boxes when you typed in your name at the beginning of this tutorial. It is important to remember to move from one text box to another by pressing the Tab key. You can also double-click on each text box to select its text for replacement. Appendix D gives more details about this dialog. Click on the OK button.

Many of the menu items have a flower-like symbol and a letter as part of the command. This means that the menu item can be selected by holding down the command key (lower left corner of keyboard) and pressing the key shown. To try this out, point to the "Apple" in the upper left corner of the screen and hold down the mouse button. Notice that the item "Help" has a command sign and a question mark (?). Release the mouse without selecting this item. Hold down the command button and type a question mark. You will need to hold down the shift key as well. The Help dialog will appear. It will open to the explanation appropriate to the subject you are exploring. Click on the Topics button to see other terms. Click on a menu name and on the Help button to get help using the program. Read the explanation for any menu item. Click on the Done button when you have explored this dialog.

Writing music with the *Explorations* Music Editor combines many of the techniques discussed above. Select New Score from the File menu. When you see a dialog appear, click OK. (You will learn about musical staves in the textbook.) When the music staves appear, the quarter note is selected (the dark square) in the Music Toolbox at the top of the screen. Move the pointer to the upper musical staff, and a quarter-note symbol appears (see Figure A–5). Click the mouse button with this note on the staff. After doing this several times, click the Play button in the Music Toolbox to hear your creation.

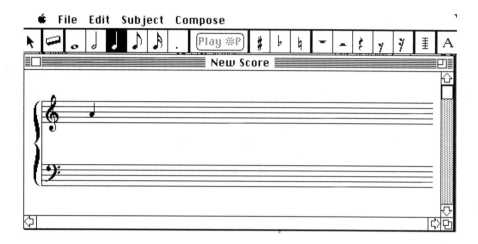

Figure A–5

To change the sound of notes, select the Pointer Tool in the upper left corner of the screen, position the tip of the arrow in the middle of the note head, and hold down the mouse button. Drag the note head to a new staff position and release the mouse button. To remove single notes, select the Eraser Tool next to the Pointer Tool and click on each individual note head. To remove a large number of notes, drag across a large area of the screen that includes all notes to be removed (see Figure A–6). After they are selected, press the Backspace or Delete key.

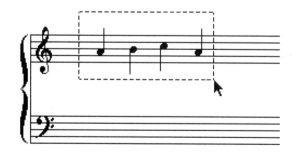

Figure A–6

The scroll bar on the right side of the window allows you to see the remaining staves on the page. Each score can be one page long and can hold ten single musical staves or five grand staves.

Scroll to the top of the page with the scroll bar and add as many notes as you like to the score. Your musical composition can be stored on any Macintosh disk. Select Save As... from the File menu. When the dialog appears, double-click on the Scores folder listed in this window. Type in a name for your musical score and click on the Save button. "First Score" is a good name. After saving your score, click in the Close Box in the upper left corner of the Subject Window.

To load a score into the computer, select Open Score... from the File menu. You will see a list of items on the disk. If the word "Scores" does not appear in the top portion of this dialog, find the Scores folder and double-click on it.

With this information you will be able to explore *Explorations* software in conjunction with the chapter exercises in this book. To set *Explorations* software for reading and exploring Chapter 1, select Note Names from the Subject menu. To stop using *Explorations* software, select Quit from the File menu.

$\mathcal{B}$ Explorations *Reference*

Opening Explorations

To start *Explorations* software, click on the *Explorations* program icon and select Open... from the File menu. Double-clicking on the *Explorations* icon has the same effect. You can also start *Explorations* software by double-clicking on a score file icon or a waveform icon. *Explorations* will automatically start and open the chosen document.

Explorations Icon   Score Icon   Waveform Icon

Using Explorations *Software in a Computer Laboratory*

In instructional laboratories it is necessary to use headphones to avoid annoying other computer users. Use portable cassette play headphones with a small plug (mini phone plug). Insert the plug in the socket marked with a loudspeaker icon on the Macintosh. To set the volume use the Control Panel.

The Four Main Explorations *Menus*

APPLE MENU

About Explorations... tells about *Explorations* software.

Help... tells how to use *Explorations* software.

The remaining items in the Apple menu are desk accessories installed in your system file; consult your system manual for further information.

FILE MENU

Most File menu items relate to writing musical scores with the Music Editor in *Explorations* software.

```
File
  New Score    ⌘N
  Open Score... ⌘O
  ─────────────────
  Close        ⌘W
  Save         ⌘S
  Save As...
  Revert to Saved
  ─────────────────
  Page Setup...
  Print...
  ─────────────────
  Report Card...
  Glossary...
  Textbook...
  ─────────────────
  Quit         ⌘Q
```

New Score opens the Music Editor and allows you to compose music. Choose to write music on five grand staves or ten single staves. These staves represent one page of music manuscript paper. *Explorations* software writes your music with correct notation as best it can. A new menu, called Compose, is added to the menu bar. You can write and edit music using the Music Toolbox and the Compose menu commands (both described below). You can save your score on disk or print it on any standard Macintosh printer.

Open Score... opens a score document on disk, for editing or printing.

Close closes the current subject window or score window. If a score window contains a score that has been changed, you will be asked whether you want to save your music on the disk. Clicking in the close box of a window has the same effect.

Save saves the latest version of an existing score on the disk under the same name.

Save As... saves your score under a new name on the disk.

Revert to saved reads the most recently saved version of your score from the disk and displays it in the window. Any changes you had made since saving that score will be lost.

Page Setup... allows you to change page parameters for your printer. See your system manual or printer manual for details.

Print... prints the score present in the score window on the chosen printer. *Explorations* software supports all standard Macintosh printers. Select a printer using the Chooser desk accessory. For high-quality laser printing, install the Sonata printer font from Adobe Corporation for use with your laser printer.

Report Card... shows a list of all tests completed and the scores you received. This is the same information that the teacher will collect from your disk. If your teacher allows you to take the tests several times, the Report Card saves only your best score for a particular test.

Glossary... gives a list of musical terms and their definitions. This glossary operates like the Help and Textbook dialogs. Click on a term in the list and its definition will appear.

Textbook... allows you to read or browse through a shorter version of this textbook. If you have already selected a subject, the explanation dialog automatically opens to the text for that subject.

Quit allows you to stop using *Explorations* software.

EDIT MENU

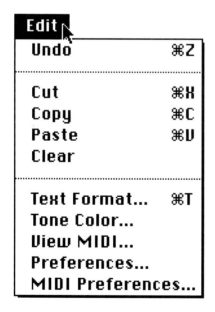

Undo reverses the last action you have taken. It allows you to reverse note or text decisions. After you Undo something, this item changes to Redo. Selecting Redo reverses the Undo process.

Cut removes selected text from a musical score and places it on the Clipboard. Select text by dragging over it with the Text Tool from the Music Toolbox.

Copy places a copy of selected text on the Clipboard.

Paste places a copy of the Clipboard's text in the document at the point where the text cursor is found.

Clear erases any selected text or music. Selected material can also be cleared by pressing the Delete or Backspace key.

Text Format... allows you to set the font, size, and style of a text block. This can be used whenever a text block is selected with the Pointer Tool or when using the Text Tool. Note that the text characteristics always apply to an entire block of text.

Tone Color... in general, this allows you to change the timbre of any sounds played through the Macintosh speaker. It is also an extensive exploratory subject in its own right (see Appendix C).

View MIDI... opens a dialog box that shows you the MIDI numbers and their meaning as you play on a MIDI keyboard. See Appendix D for details.

Preferences... allows you to determine certain characteristics of your learning environment. For example, you may wish to establish a practice session made up of descending intervals only. If you would rather not be notified that you've made a mistake during a test, you can turn off the beep that normally occurs.

MIDI Preferences... allows you to set items that control your MIDI instrument. In order to play music with a MIDI instrument, select Play MIDI. You can set the MIDI channel and Macintosh interface port used to play music. Individual MIDI keys can be established to play metronome clicks for use in the Rhythm subject.

SUBJECT MENU

Subject
Note Names
Rhythm

Scales
Key Signatures
Melody

Intervals
Triads
7th Chords

Chord Function

This menu contains a list of subjects available in *Explorations* software. When you select a subject from this menu, a window opens in which you can explore that subject. There are no rules for explorations—just try things and see what happens. Individual chapters in this book give suggestions for exploring each subject. When a subject is open, a new menu, named after the subject, is placed in the menu bar. This new menu contains options appropriate to the subject you have chosen.

Any number of subjects can be opened simultaneously. Individual subject windows and menus are described at the beginning of each chapter in which a subject is introduced in this textbook.

Instructional Format for Explorations Software

Explorations combines a Music Editor for writing musical scores with instructional materials divided into subjects. The File and Edit menus are used to open and manipulate your musical scores. The Compose menu is added to the menu bar to assist in this process.

There are three principal activities within each subject. These activities allow you to explore the materials, practice basic skills, and test your musical knowledge.

Explore   allows you to experiment with the musical elements of a subject. You can write notes, play keyboards, and enter musical labels while the computer responds to your actions with sound and analytical remarks. Each chapter of this book suggests activities for exploration that introduce and demonstrate musical concepts.

Practice   allows you to practice written, aural, and keyboard skills. All practice sessions use the same format as tests in each subject, except (1) you are allowed to try more than one answer, (2) you are given hints after wrong answers, and (3) you are allowed to give up and see the answer. Details vary among subjects and methods; types of practice sessions are discussed in the section *Practice Sessions and Test Types*, later in this appendix. In addition to practicing for specific tests, you can design your own practice sessions to fine-tune particular skills. Select Practice again to change your practice environment. To stop practicing a subject, select Explore or Test from the selected subject menu or click on the close box of the subject window.

Test   tests your skills in the selected subject. Each test has anywhere from ten to sixty questions. Your percentage scores are written on your disk for your teacher to collect later. Details vary among subjects and entry methods; types of tests are discussed in *Practice Sessions and Test Types*. To stop a test in progress, select Explore or Practice from the subject's individual menu or click on the close box of the Subject Window. No scores are stored for tests that are not completed.

The Music Toolbox

The Music Editor and all subjects use the Music Toolbox. Its tools allow you to enter music notation using the mouse. You can move the Music Toolbox to any part of the screen by holding the option key while dragging the toolbox with the pointer tool.

Pointer Tool

allows you to move musical symbols or to select them for special operations, such as beaming and tying notes. Click with the *tip* of the Pointer Tool positioned on a note head, barline, or text block to select it. Shift-click to add another item to the selection. Drag an item to move it. When you move a note, hold down the Shift key before dragging to restrain movement to horizontal only. If you move any note in a chord horizontally, the remaining notes of the chord will move to the same position when the mouse button is released. If you draw a dotted rectangle (by dragging with the Pointer Tool) in the score, everything inside the rectangle will be selected. Note, however, that barlines or text blocks must be completely enclosed in order to select them; if this can't be done without selecting unwanted material, use the shift-click method to add items individually to the selection. The entire selection can be deleted by pressing the Delete key. To cancel a selection, click elsewhere in the Score window or in the Music Toolbox. **Special feature**: While using any tool, you can use the pointer tool temporarily by holding down the command key (the key with the Apple on it). When the command key is released, the previously chosen tool resumes.

Eraser Tool

allows you to delete notes, barlines, text blocks, or time signatures. Position the cursor with its diagonal line on the item to be deleted and click the mouse button.

Note Tools

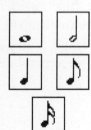

allow you to add notes of the corresponding rhythmic value on the staff. The stem direction is determined automatically by the Music Editor. All notes receive implied accidentals from the key signature that can be altered, using the accidental tools (see next page). Notes added above or below existing notes of the same value will share stems with those notes. If you click above or below a note of a different value, the Music Editor may change the stem direction of one or both notes to avoid notation errors.

Dot Tool

converts whole-, half-, quarter-, or eighth-note tools into tools for adding dotted notes. You must already have a note tool selected when you choose the dot. Dots cannot be added individually to notes in the score. Existing notes become dotted values by deleting the note, choosing note and dot tools, and replacing the note with the new value. Clicking anywhere in the Music Toolbox turns off the dot tool.

Play Button

plays the musical score displayed in the Subject Window. While music is playing, the name of the button changes to Stop. Click on this button again to stop the music. The Play button in the Music Toolbox always plays the results of *your* musical actions. In ear-training practice sessions and tests, a Replay button allows you to hear exercises composed by the computer.

Accidental Tools

allow you to add or remove an accidental from an existing note within common rules of musical notation. Position the accidental properly on the staff, just to the left of the note, and click the mouse. Clicking with the Sharp Tool to the left of a sharped note converts its accidental to a double sharp. Clicking with the Flat Tool to the left of a note head with a flat converts its accidental to a double flat. If the note's accidental is found in the current key signature, the accidental is *not* displayed. Note: These tools have a slightly different function in the Key Signatures subject (see Chapter 4).

Rest Tools

function just like Note Tools but add rests to the music.

Barline Tools

allow you to add barlines and double barlines to your score. Select this tool by clicking on the Barline icon in the Music Toolbox. Your cursor becomes a vertical line. Clicking anywhere on a staff adds a barline at that place. Barlines can be added before or after existing notes and text or placed on the staff before you write your music. Clicking a second time on the Barline icon changes the icon to a double bar and allows you to place a double bar in your score—for example, at the end of a piece. Clicking in any part of the Music Toolbox reinstates a single barline in the Barline Tool icon.

Text Tool

allows you to enter titles, lyrics, and other text in your compositions. Click above, below, or between staves to establish the position of your text. A flashing insertion point will appear. Type any text you wish. You can use the I-beam cursor to select text for cutting, copying, or pasting, as in any Macintosh application. You can move the entire text block by dragging it with the Pointer Tool. To change the style of the text, click with the Text Tool and select Text Format from the Edit menu.

Practice Sessions and Test Types

Practice sessions and tests help firmly establish musical skills developed by exploration and reading. Formats for these exercises can be divided into two skill areas: Written Theory Skills and Ear-Training Skills. In each skill area, three possible entry methods are used to answer questions.

Written Theory Skills	*Ear-Training Skills*
Write Music	ET Write Music
Analyze Music	ET Analyze Music
Keyboard	ET Keyboard

For each subject's tests or practice sessions you must select one of these skill areas, but not all tests use all entry methods. Here is a general description of each entry method, although the details may vary for certain subjects:

Write Music

ET Write Music

Questions are answered by adding musical notation to the staff using the Music Toolbox. In this format the name of a musical structure is given or, in Ear Training, a musical structure is played. Generally the first note is given and you must add the remaining notes and accidentals to complete the requested structure. When you are done, click the Ready button.

In a practice session, you can alter incorrect answers as often as you wish or click the Give Up button to see the answer. Incorrect answers can be altered by dragging notes with the Pointer Tool or by changing accidentals with the Accidental Tools. You can also click the Start Over button and begin again. After arriving at the correct answer, continue by clicking the Next button (this feature can be altered within the Preferences dialog, selectable from the Edit menu).

Analyze Music
ET Analyze Music

In this format, the written notation or, in Ear Training, played example is provided. Your task is to enter the proper analysis label for the required musical structure. For example, you might be asked to identify a major scale or a particular type of seventh chord. Enter your answer by clicking choices in the Entry Window at the bottom of the screen. Click the Enter button when you have constructed your answer.

Keyboard
ET Keyboard

The screen keyboard will open automatically for this type of activity, but you may use your MIDI instrument if you wish. Enter your answers by clicking or playing keyboard notes. Often one or more notes will be provided (grayed on the screen keyboard). As soon as you have played enough keys to form an answer, the computer evaluates that answer. If you discover an error during your entry, click the Start Over button and begin again.

In the **Rhythm** practice sessions and tests, the keyboard activities are replaced with playing rhythms on the computer's spacebar or on any MIDI key.

This figure shows a sample practice session dialog where you choose your subject matter and type of activity. Notice that the filled diamond indicates that a test is also available for a particular subject area. Those without diamonds are practice sessions that prepare you for that level. Choose a practice

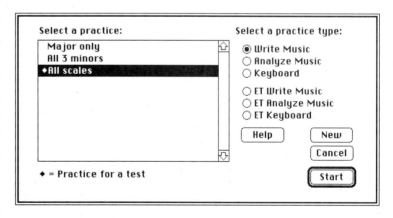

session by clicking on its name in the list, choose one of the radio buttons for the entry method, and click the Start button. The Help button provides a description of the six test types, in case you forget. Click the New button whenever you wish to design your own practice session. This allows you to customize your practice by choosing specific musical structures to meet your music learning needs.

Tone Color Dialog

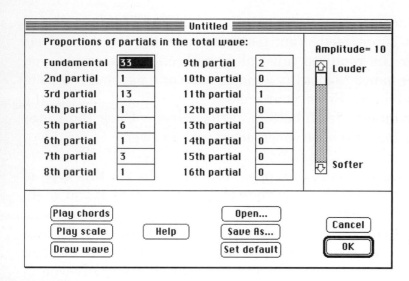

Proportions of partials in the total wave:					Amplitude= 10
Fundamental	33	9th partial	2	
2nd partial	1	10th partial	0	
3rd partial	13	11th partial	1	
4th partial	1	12th partial	0	
5th partial	6	13th partial	0	
6th partial	1	14th partial	0	
7th partial	3	15th partial	0	
8th partial	1	16th partial	0	

Appendix C gives an introduction to musical acoustics. This dialog is accessed by selecting Tone Color... from the Edit menu. It allows you to experiment with different combinations of waveforms and is thus another exploratory subject. Unlike other subjects, however, you can't go back and forth between Tone Color and other subjects by selecting from the menus; you can leave Tone Color by clicking Cancel or OK.

Don't be put off by the amount of information shown in this dialog. You don't have to learn everything at once. Read Appendix C carefully when exploring this material.

Text boxes   contain numbers that represent the relative strengths of various partials in the total sound. Partials are the different frequencies present in a sound.

Amplitude   is the strength with which air molecules are disturbed. Listeners perceive this strength as volume. This scroll bar affects the size of the wave, both when it's drawn and when it's played. If you set it to zero, you will get no sound. The loudness of the Macintosh speaker, which corresponds to the maximum amplitude, is determined by the volume control in the Control Panel desk accessory. For best results set the Macintosh Control Panel Volume Control to its highest setting.

Play chords   allows you to hear a series of chords using the waves you create.

Play scale   allows you to hear single notes in a scale using the waves you create. This scale plays very high and very low to demonstrate how your wave will sound in all ranges.

Draw Wave   opens a second window and draws one period of the total wave based on the relative strengths of the partials you have specified. It may take a few seconds to calculate, however. When you're finished looking at the picture, just click the mouse.

Help   provides on-line instructions on how to operate this dialog.

Open   loads a previously saved wave from the disk. *Explorations* comes supplied with a number of sample waves that you will want to look at and listen to.

Save as...   stores the current wave information as a file on the disk. You may then open the wave any time you want to use it in the future; or double-click on the wave file to start the program next time; or share it with your friends. Give each wave a name that reflects its character.

Set Default   sets the numbers and waveform to values for the standard wave that *Explorations* normally uses when the program starts.

OK   closes the dialog and sets the wave you last created as the sound for playing music through the Macintosh speaker. This change of timbre lasts until you quit the program. If you want to use the same wave during your next session, save it and start the program next time by double-clicking on its icon.

Cancel   closes the dialog without changing the tone color.

Problems and Solutions

Problem   *Explorations* will not play any sound, or is very quiet, on my Macintosh speaker or in my headphones.

Solutions   Make sure Play Mac is selected in the MIDI Preferences dialog.

Make sure the volume control in the Control Panel desk accessory isn't set to zero.

See if the Amplitude setting in the Tone Color dialog is set too low.

Problem   I'm hearing no sound from my MIDI instrument.

Solutions   Make sure Play MIDI is selected in the MIDI Preferences dialog.

Recheck the connections and wires to make sure they are assembled correctly.

Is your instrument turned on and plugged in (if appropriate)? Check your instrument's volume control. Does your instrument require headphones or an external amplifier?

Was your MIDI connected when the Macintosh was started up? If not, quit *Explorations*. When you have returned to the Macintosh desktop, select Restart from the Special menu.

What channel does your instrument expect to receive data on? Consult your instrument's user manual to find out. Set the channel in the MIDI Preferences dialog box.

Problem   A chord or note collides with the accidentals of the next chord.

Solution   Move the second chord further to the right on the screen. All accidentals will move with the notes.

Problem   When combining notes of different values, the editor can often show the following notation.

The notation shown occurs because the Music Editor cannot guess the user's intentions for distributing notes among voices. Assuming that both the A and the E belong to the upper voice, the E should be written with the stem up. It could also be true that the user will add another eighth note in the upper voice above the F and that the lower voice leaps from F up to E.

Solutions   Select the second eighth note and select Flip Stem from the Compose menu.
Selecting the two eighth notes and selecting Beam Notes from the Compose menu will also solve this problem.

C Musical Sound

For computer activities in this chapter, select Tone Color... from the Edit menu. In addition to the materials in this chapter, you may wish to read the description of this dialog found in Appendix B.

Sounds are created whenever air particles that make up our atmosphere are disturbed—that is, when they are pressed together (**compression**) and pulled apart (**rarefaction**). These air disturbances can repeat in regular patterns called **tones** or can form irregular patterns called **noise**.

A repeated pattern of compressions and rarefactions is called **vibration**. A vibrating string produces sound by moving first in one direction and then in the opposite direction. Pulses of air are pushed into a wind instrument by the vibration of a reed or the opening and closing of a brass player's lips. Voltages push or pull a loudspeaker to disturb the air around it.

We can draw a graphic image of this process of compression and rarefaction. Figure C–1 represents air pressure changes for a sine wave, the simplest of musical sounds.

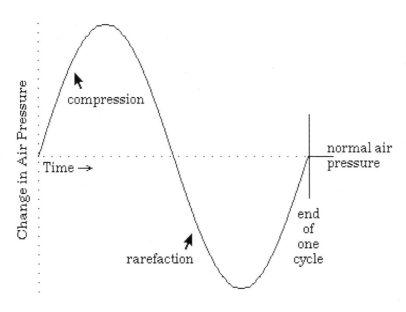

Figure C–1

The greater the disturbance of the air, the louder the sound. The loudness of the sound is called **amplitude** and is represented vertically on waveform graphs. The greater the amplitude of the sound, the higher the waveform is drawn. In Figure C–2 there are two waveforms. The first of these is louder than the second.

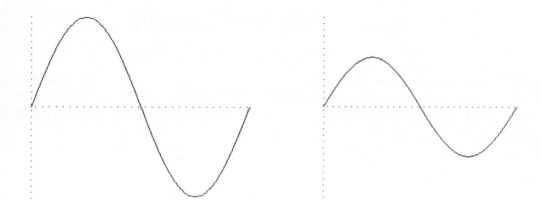

Figure C–2

Click on the Open button and open "Sine Wave" from the Waves folder. After the waveform is loaded, click on the Draw Waveform button. After a few seconds, the waveform will appear on the screen. A single mouse click returns you to the dialog. Click on the Play Scale button and hear the waveform. Change the Amplitude scroll bar in the upper right portion of the screen by clicking in the gray portion, draw the waveform again, and hear it played. Notice how the change in amplitude alters the sound and its waveform.

The waveform in Figure C–1 represents one compression and one rarefaction, that is, one complete **cycle** of a sine wave. **Frequency** is the number of times per second a sound source vibrates back and forth, that is, the number of cycles per second. The greater the frequency, the higher the tone. Generally the size of an acoustical instrument determines how high or low it will sound in relation to others. Flutes play higher sounds than tubas, violins play higher than cellos, and so on.

Graphic waveforms can also show relative frequency. Figure C–3 shows two waveforms. The second waveform represents a tone that has a frequency twice as high as the first. Two cycles of the wave are represented for the same amount of time as the single cycle of the first wave.

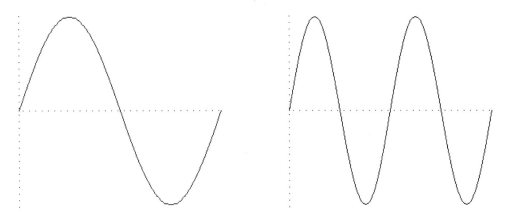

Figure C–3

Humans with normal hearing can hear vibrations between twenty and twenty thousand cycles per second. Acoustical instruments play notes in a small portion of that range. For example, tones played on a piano have a range of approximately thirty to four thousand cycles per second. The eardrum starts to vibrate as disturbed air molecules come in contact with it. This process causes other parts of the ear to vibrate, and the resulting electrical impulses are transmitted to the brain. Our minds recognize sounds around us based on previous experience as listeners. Humans tend to appreciate familiar musical sounds and styles. Music study can open new doors to unfamiliar musical sounds.

The **fundamental** is the frequency on which a tone is based. For example, the A above middle C has a fundamental of 440—that is, a frequency of 440 cycles per second (designated as A-440). Orchestras use this frequency as a common **pitch** to tune their instruments before a concert. Pitches are the particular frequencies chosen from all possible frequencies for making music. If instrumentalists and singers match these chosen frequencies closely enough, they are "in tune" with the other members of an ensemble.

One way in which sounds are different from one another is by their tone color, or **timbre**. Sine waves are simple waveforms because they contain only one frequency, but most sounds are combinations of many frequencies, called **partials**. In spite of the presence of these partials, we hear most sounds as complete units rather than as a collection of individual frequencies.

Using the computer, we can set the relative strengths of different partials in order to hear and see individual frequencies present in a waveform. Notice that numbers for the Sine Wave are all zeros except the "fundamental." Click on the Draw Wave button to review the shape of a Sine Wave. (Click the mouse to return to the dialog.)

Enter a 0 (zero) in the fundamental text box and a 1 for the second partial. Click on the Draw Wave button and notice that the second partial has twice the number of cycles shown. Click the mouse to return to the dialog; then enter a 0 for the second partial and a 1 in the third partial text box. Click on the Draw Wave button and see that the third partial has three cycles shown in the same space on the graph. Do the same for the fourth partial.

The number used to describe each partial indicates its number of cycles per second in relation to the fundamental. The second partial is twice the frequency of the fundamental, the third partial is three times the frequency of the fundamental, and so on.

Generally the fundamental is the strongest partial; others are weaker and vary in relative strength. The pitch of the sound is established by its fundamental, and the timbre is determined by the relative strengths of the upper partials. Upper partials for clarinets have different strengths than do those for violins. This accounts for the difference in their timbres.

Enter a 1 for both the fundamental and the sixteenth partial, entering 0 for all other partials. This establishes the sixteenth partial and the fundamental as equally strong. Such a sound is possible only with electronic instruments. Acoustical instruments never have a sixteenth partial that is equal in strength to the fundamental.

Click on the Play Scale button to hear this timbre. Notice that you can hear two distinct frequencies of the wave; the fundamental is the lower of these two pitches. View the waveform for this pair of frequencies. Notice how the presence of a strong sixteenth partial changes the shape of the sine wave.

Now enter 20 in the text box for the fundamental. This makes the fundamental twenty times stronger than the sixteenth partial. (Remember, these numbers and resulting waves represent *relative* strengths of the partials.) Playing the scale again will reveal the higher frequency to be much softer because its relative strength is diminished and it becomes part of the total sound. View the waveform for this new sound. The weaker sixteenth partial makes less pronounced air pressure changes.

The potential upper partials for acoustical musical instruments follow a particular pattern. The notes shown in Figure C–4 represent the pitches that are closest to the frequencies present in a low C. Partials 1, 2, 4, 8, and 16 are the note C in various octaves. Each successive C is an octave higher than the previous C, and each partial number for a C is twice that of the previous C. As seen earlier, the ratios of the partial numbers are the same as the ratios of frequencies of the upper partials.

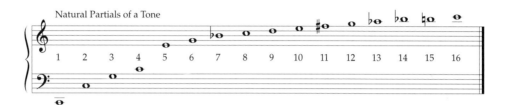

Figure C–4

Enter a 1 into the text box for partials 1, 2, 4, 8, and 16 and enter 0 for all other partials. When you click the Play Scale button, you will find that the results sound like notes played in several octaves at the same time. When we give these partials relative strengths more similar to most acoustical instruments, their individuality fades. Enter 50 for the fundamental, 10 for the second partial, and 1 for the fourth, eighth, and sixteenth partials. This ratio produces a sound more like a single tone. View its waveform and experiment with other values for these partials.

Waveforms are provided on your *Explorations* disk. Some of these imitate the sounds of acoustical instruments. These are only approximations and do not consistently sound like these instruments, for two reasons:

1. The Macintosh speaker capabilities do not allow extremely accurate reproduction of these waveforms. The speaker cannot imitate all aspects of the sound, such as the way in which a performer attacks a note.
2. Waveforms for acoustical instruments change depending on the particular range in which an instrument is playing. Performers also change the sound while a note is played. Listen to fine violinists or jazz saxophonists. Pay careful attention to how they shape the sound of each note.

As you experiment with various combinations of partials, some particularly pleasing or quite obnoxious sounds will result (hear and draw "Spike" on your *Explorations* disk). You may wish to save the most interesting of these on your disk. You will find that relatively strong upper partials produce a greater contrast in the waveform patterns and harsher tones through the Macintosh speaker. Any timbre you design and save to disk can be used in *Explorations* Explore, Practice, and Test activities. Simply click on Save when you have a timbre you want to keep and give the sound a name you can remember easily. Load this timbre using the Tone Color dialog each time you use *Explorations* or double-click on the icon for that waveform each time you start up the program.

All sounds are produced by air disturbances. Musical sounds are those air disturbances that are intended for musical experiences. Our musical experiences enable us to recognize familiar musical sounds and distinguish them from one another. Casual listeners can easily learn to recognize the difference between the tone qualities of various instruments after listening and comparing their sounds. Performers must learn to recognize subtle differences in pitches in order to play "in tune." Conductors and other musical leaders must pay close attention to articulation and interpretation to be sure the ensemble is performing in an appropriate manner. Such aural skills are very important for all musicians.

Summary

1. Sound is created by disturbances of air particles to which our ears and minds respond.
2. Regular patterns of vibration (compression and rarefaction) produce specific frequencies.
3. Musical pitches are frequencies we use to make music, chosen from all possible frequencies.
4. When instruments play, our perception of any pitch is based on the fundamental frequency. Their tone color or timbre is based on the combination and relative strengths of upper partials, other frequencies present in the sound.
5. The numbers for a sound's partials show the relationship between the frequencies of those partials. For example, the frequency of the third partial is three times the frequency of the fundamental.

Here are some useful experiments you can perform to demonstrate musical sounds and timbre.

Exercise 1: Find an acoustical piano and open its lid. Holding down the sustaining pedal (the one on the right), shout "hey!" into the instrument. (Actually, any word will do.) Listen to the strings vibrate. This occurs because the frequencies in the sound of your voice cause any strings that share one of those frequencies to vibrate sympathetically. Any string will vibrate when air disturbances corresponding to its frequency hit the string. Try different words with high and low sounds. Sing a constant pitch into the piano to activate strings corresponding to the partials of your chosen pitch.

Exercise 2: Another demonstration of the presence of upper partials can be accomplished on an acoustical piano. Silently push down the piano keys for middle C, the G below middle C, and the E above middle C. (Middle C is not only in the middle of the staff but also located in the middle of keyboards with eighty-eight keys.) Play the C found two octaves below middle C. Play this tone loudly and quickly, and listen as the strings for G, C, and E vibrate sympathetically with the third, fourth, and fifth partials of the low C. These strings are responding to the frequencies of upper partials for the low C that you played. Because their frequencies are the same as those upper partials, they are set in motion by those regular air disturbances.

Exercise 3: Ask a French horn or trombone player to play a "pedal tone" for you. This tone is the fundamental of that instrument. Then ask him or her to play up the overtone series for you. Look at Figure C–4 while you listen and see that these notes can all be played by the instrumentalist. Changing the slide on the trombone or changing the valves on the horn changes the length of the instrument and forces the player's air to travel a longer or shorter distance. With each length of tubing the player can produce a similar harmonic series on a different note.

Exercise 4: Ask a string player to play some "harmonics." To do this he or she will touch the strings lightly. Touching the string in the middle divides it in half, and the sound produced is an octave higher than the frequency of the string. Touching the string on one-quarter of its length yields a tone two octaves higher than the string's pitch.

Use these worksheets for a written record of numbers used to construct your favorite tone colors (timbres).

Proportions of partials in the total wave:

Fundamental
2nd partial
3rd partial
4th partial
5th partial
6th partial
7th partial
8th partial
9th partial
10th partial
11th partial
12th partial
13th partial
14th partial
15th partial
16th partial

Proportions of partials in the total wave:

Fundamental
2nd partial
3rd partial
4th partial
5th partial
6th partial
7th partial
8th partial
9th partial
10th partial
11th partial
12th partial
13th partial
14th partial
15th partial
16th partial

Proportions of partials in the total wave:

Fundamental
2nd partial
3rd partial
4th partial
5th partial
6th partial
7th partial
8th partial
9th partial
10th partial
11th partial
12th partial
13th partial
14th partial
15th partial
16th partial

Proportions of partials in the total wave:

Fundamental
2nd partial
3rd partial
4th partial
5th partial
6th partial
7th partial
8th partial
9th partial
10th partial
11th partial
12th partial
13th partial
14th partial
15th partial
16th partial

Proportions of partials in the total wave:

Fundamental
2nd partial
3rd partial
4th partial
5th partial
6th partial
7th partial
8th partial
9th partial
10th partial
11th partial
12th partial
13th partial
14th partial
15th partial
16th partial

Proportions of partials in the total wave:

Fundamental
2nd partial
3rd partial
4th partial
5th partial
6th partial
7th partial
8th partial
9th partial
10th partial
11th partial
12th partial
13th partial
14th partial
15th partial
16th partial

$\mathcal{D}$ MIDI

MIDI (Musical Instrument Digital Interface) is a set of methods for communicating musical data between two or more synthesizers or between synthesizers and computers. *Explorations* software allows you to explore subjects, practice, take tests, and hear your musical compositions using a MIDI instrument. You can also play notes into the music editor to produce scores. Many low-cost MIDIs and MIDI-compatible instruments are available on the market today.

In order to make use of MIDI with *Explorations,* you will need the following items:

- A MIDI for your Macintosh, plugged into the Modem Port
- A MIDI-compatible keyboard synthesizer
- Two MIDI cables

These items are available at local music stores, department stores, and computer mail-order companies. Choose a synthesizer with the features you want within the price range you can afford. There is a wide range of styles and features. Shop around!

Exploring MIDI

When you have the necessary hardware assembled, plug the MIDI (the interface hardware) into the Modem Port of your Macintosh. Plug one of the MIDI cables into the MIDI-In socket of the MIDI and into the MIDI-Out socket of your synthesizer. Plug the other MIDI cable into the MIDI-Out socket of the MIDI and the MIDI-In socket of your synthesizer. Open *Explorations* software and select MIDI Preferences... from the Edit menu. You will see the dialog shown in Figure D–1.

The "Music on Mac," "Music on MIDI now," and "Music on MIDI always" radio buttons choose the method for playing music. If you always want to use a MIDI instrument for playing music, click on "Music on MIDI always." This will establish your synthesizer as your sound source every time you start using *Explorations*. If you wish to use a synthesizer only once, click on "Music on MIDI now." With this button set, your computer will play music on the Mac speaker next time you use *Explorations* software. The Music MIDI Channel is the number of the MIDI channel you wish to use to play back musical examples in *Explorations*. You may select any one of sixteen channels to send the MIDI data to your synthesizer. Most synthesizers are set at the factory to receive on Channel 1, but this can usually be changed. Check your synthesizer's user manual for details.

The playback method used for the metronome can be set separately from the music playback. Very often MIDI users will use a set of percussion instruments in order to play the metronome. Select "MIDI now" or "MIDI always" as you did for music playback. Consult your synthesizer user manual and establish a channel number for playing percussion instruments (most often Channel 10). Enter that number in the Metronome MIDI channel text box. Enter MIDI numbers for particular percussion instruments provided in your synthesizer manual. Try a low-sounding instrument for the downbeats, a higher sound for the beats, and the highest sound for the subdivisions. Explore several sounds until you find the metronome you like.

Click on the OK button to close the dialog, select any subject, and click on the Play button. You should hear the music through audio speakers or through headphones connected to your synthesizer.

MIDI Preferences

○ Music on Mac speaker   ◉ Metronome on Mac speaker
◉ Music on MIDI now   ○ Metronome on MIDI now
○ Music on MIDI always   ○ Metronome on MIDI always

Metronome MIDI numbers:

Subdivisions: 84
Beats: 83
Downbeats: 82

Music MIDI channel: [1]   Metronome MIDI channel: [1]

Interface speed: 1.0 MHz (Standard)   [Cancel]

MIDI connected to: Modem Port   [OK]

Figure D–1

How MIDI Works

The MIDI Specification, published by the MIDI Manufacturers Association, describes both hardware and communications protocol for transmitting data from one MIDI device to another. Once your hardware is properly installed, your MIDI devices will automatically speak a common language to each other.

Select View MIDI... from the Edit menu. When the View MIDI dialog box is displayed, click on the Check Box labeled, "Note on/note off only." Then hold down middle C for about 2 seconds. Then play a shorter note on the E above middle C. The results should be similar to those shown in Figure D–2.

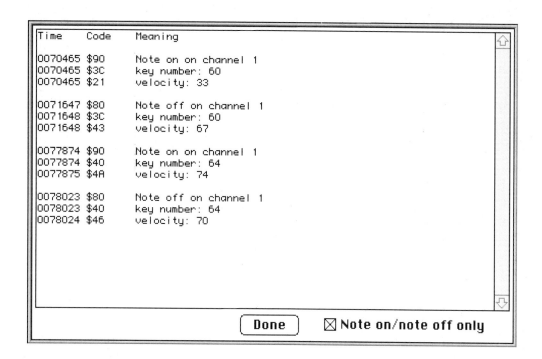

Figure D–2

You will notice three columns in the dialog box. The Time column contains information obtained from the Macintosh clock. This is the number of Mac clock ticks since the time you turned on your computer (60 ticks per second). This information allows software to determine the relative timing between MIDI events. The Code column contains the actual MIDI data that were transmitted by your computer. The Meaning column tells you *Explorations* software's definition of each MIDI number in the Code column.

It is important to remember that these numbers represent performance data and not sound. MIDI communicates the mechanical functions of playing music, such as, keyboard keys, sliders, pitch wheels, and their movements. For example, MIDI sends the number of a tone color you have chosen on your synthesizer, but not the actual sound that the chosen tone color produces through your speaker system.

The MIDI language is made up of numbers from zero (0) through 255 which can be represented in one byte of computer data (eight bits). These numbers are shown as Hexadecimal numbers ($00-$FF), a standard computer representation of numbers ("$" indicates such a number). Numbers from $80-$FF (128-255) are used as **Command Bytes**, or **Status Bytes**, numbers that establish the type of message to be sent. Each Status Byte is followed by one or more **Data Bytes,** which give the details of each message. In the Code column of Figure D–2, the Status Byte $90 indicates that a key was pressed on Channel 1. The two Data Bytes that follow ($3C and $21) tell which key (middle C, MIDI key number 60) it was and its velocity—that is, how fast that key went down. In the following group of numbers, the Status Byte $80 indicates that a key was released on Channel 1. The following two Data Bytes indicate that it was MIDI key number 60 and the velocity of its release.

Figure D–3 contains another method for turning on and off notes that your synthesizer might use. Notice that to turn off the note, the synthesizer sent a $90 (Note on) with a velocity of zero. That has the same meaning in MIDI protocol as Note off ($80). However, this method does not allow the numbers to indicate how fast the key was released. This can be useful information to give an accurate end to a sound.

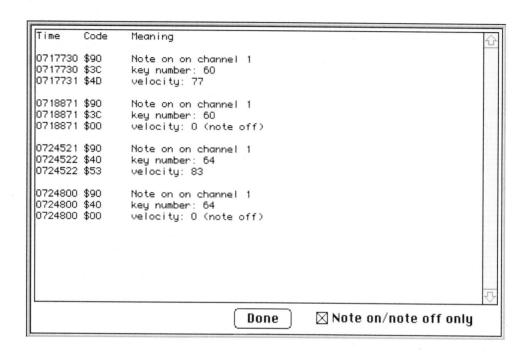

Figure D–3

Note on and Note off are two examples of one category of MIDI data called "Channel Messages." The data sent through channel messages specify the channel (1-16) on which a message is to be sent and received. The categories of channel messages are shown in Figure D–4. The computer number (hexadecimal), its decimal number equivalent, and the definition of each Status Byte are given.

Hex	Dec	Definition
$80	128	Note off
$90	144	Note on (with zero velocity, Note off)
$A0	160	Polyphonic Key Pressure (Aftertouch for each key independently)
$B0	176	Control Change (changes in volume, expression, effects, etc.)
$C0	192	Program Change (change of patch number or sound)
$D0	208	Channel Pressure (Aftertouch for all keys)
$E0	224	Pitch Bend Change
$F0	240	System Exclusive (info that only one synthesizer understands)

Figure D-4

Uncheck the check box at the bottom of the View MIDI dialog box and explore all the controls on your synthesizer to see the results. Move the pitch wheel, push buttons, change the sound, and play notes. Notice each Status Byte and the Data Bytes that follow it. *Explorations* software shows you the definition of each set of numbers. You can also scroll back to an earlier event to compare it with new events.

Each Status Byte is followed by at least one Data Byte. The Data Bytes will mean different things depending on the Status Byte and its definition. Figure D–5 indicates the meanings of Data Bytes based on their preceding Status Byte.

Status Byte	Data	Data
Note off	Key Number	Velocity
Note on	Key Number	Velocity (If 0, then Note off)
Aftertouch	Key Number	Pressure Value
Control Change	Controller Number	Controller Value
Program Change	Program Value	
Channel Pressure	Pressure Value	
Pitch Bend	Pitch Bend Value	Pitch Bend Value
System Exclusive	Series of Data Bytes with info for a particular synthesizer.	

Figure D-5

MIDI protocol is a simple language, but the number of details makes it seem complicated. That is why we use machines to deal with these details. The fact that computers and synthesizers communicate with some degree of compatibility allows humans to concentrate on the music to be made and leave the details of communicating the associated performance data to the machines.

For further information on MIDI, two useful Websites to visit are
MIDI Manufacturers Association—http://www2.midi.org/mma/
Harmony Central—http://www.harmony-central.com/MIDI/

$\mathscr{E}$ *Chord Qualities and Inversions*

This appendix contains a list of the principal chord qualities for triads and seventh chords (see Figure E–1), followed by a table of chord inversions and labels to describe them (see Figure E–2). Pop chord symbols show the root and quality of the chord and indicate if the bass note is not the root of the chord. Figured bass numbers reflect the essential intervals of notes above the lowest voice of the chord.

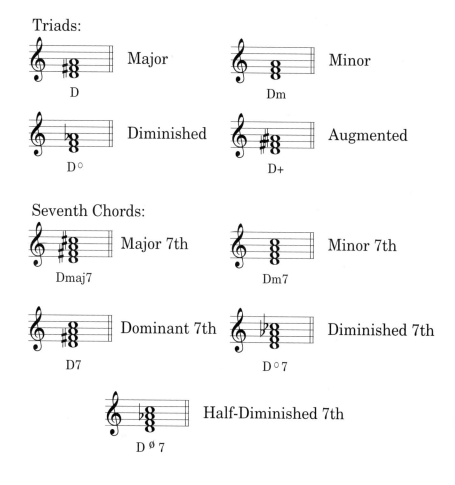

Figure E–1

Chord Inversions:		Pop Chord Symbol	Figured Bass No.
Root Position		Dm	5 3 or no figures
1st Inversion		Dm/F	6 3 or 6
2nd Inversion		Dm/A	6 4
Root Position		Dm7	7
1st Inversion		Dm7/F	6 5
2nd Inversion		Dm7/A	4 3
3rd Inversion		Dm7/C	4 2 or 2

Figure E–2

ℱ *Piano Scale Fingerings*

All major and minor key signatures and their scales are listed in this appendix. In the minor scales, the melodic minor form is used. Learn to play these scales on a keyboard instrument. Some may seem difficult at first, but with practice your skill will increase. Learn one hand, then the other, and finally play them with both hands. The numbers above or below the staff indicate the finger that should be used to play each note. The thumb of each hand is finger number 1, each index finger is number 2, and so on. Practice these scales slowly at first, concentrating on accuracy and a constant beat.

Major Scales

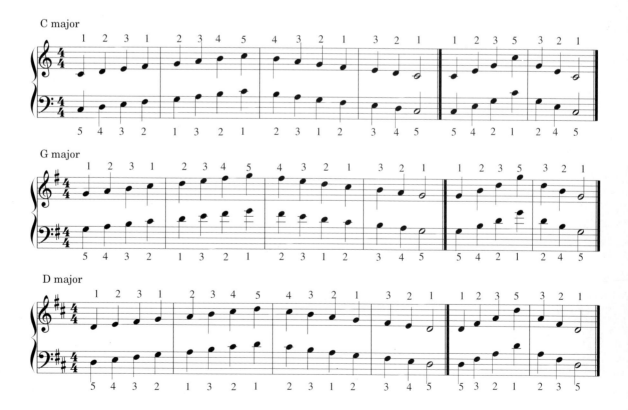

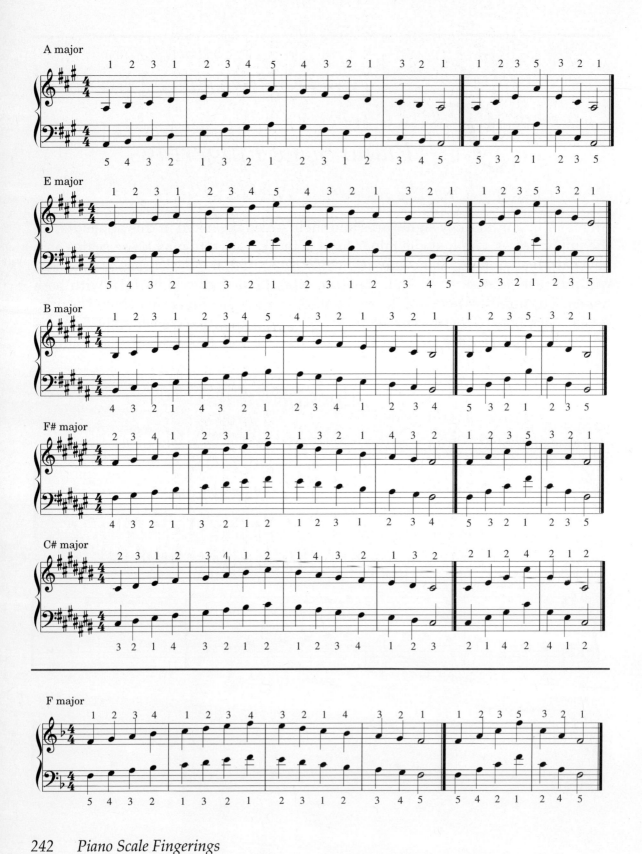

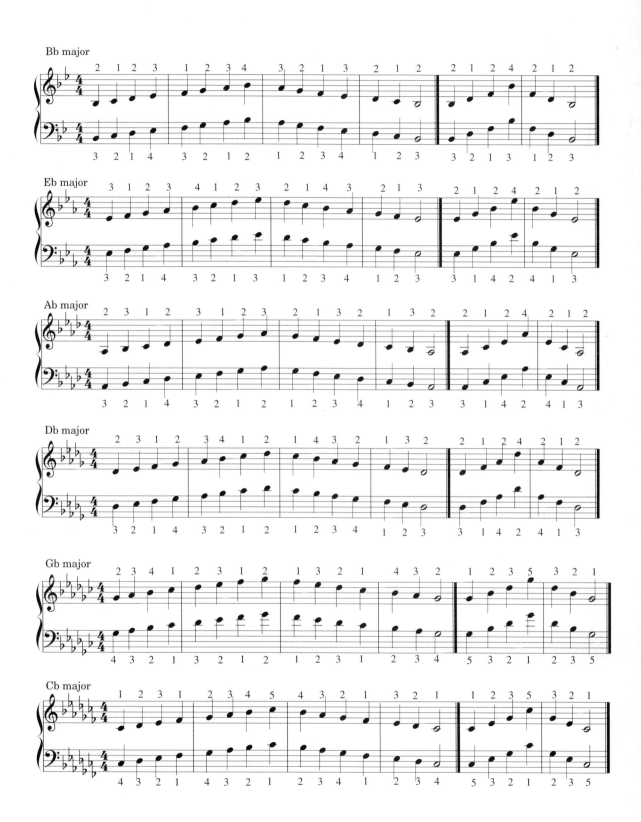

Minor Scales

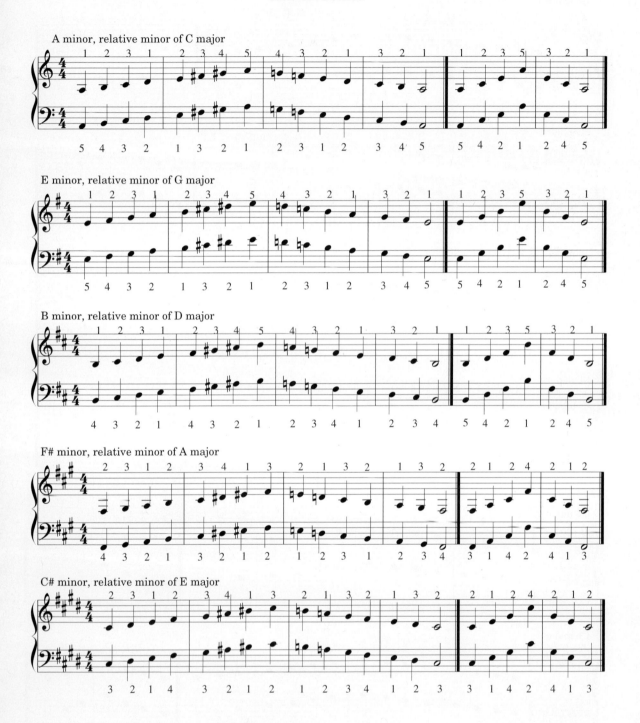

G# minor, relative minor of B major

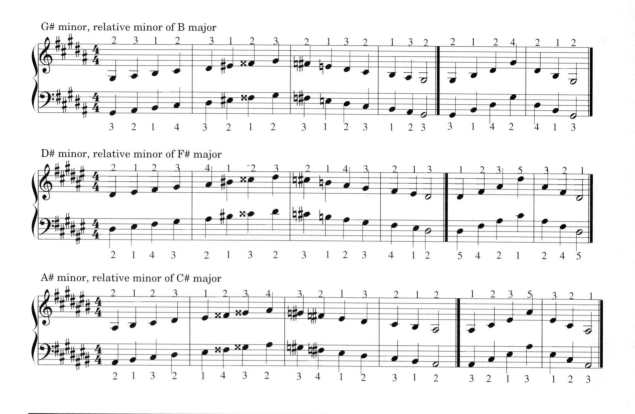

D# minor, relative minor of F# major

A# minor, relative minor of C# major

D minor, relative minor of F major

G minor, relative minor of Bb major

C minor, relative minor of Eb major

F minor, relative minor of Ab major

Bb minor, relative minor of Gb major

Eb minor, relative minor of Gb major

Ab minor, relative minor of Cb major

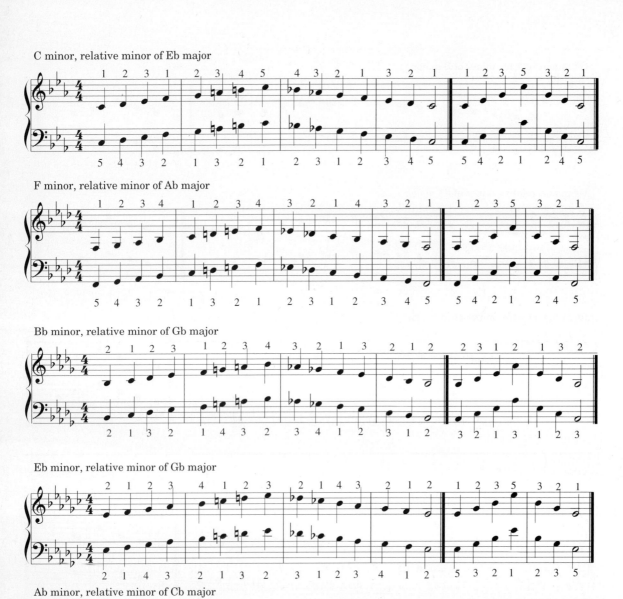

G Guitar Tuning and Chords

In addition to standard music notation, guitarists are often asked to read chord charts as shown on the following pages. For centuries, guitar symbols have been used to represent notes played by guitarists.

Explorations software allows you to explore this notation within the Triads and 7th Chords subjects by selecting Guitar from the selected Subject menu.

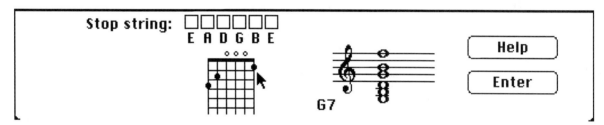

When the Guitar Window opens, it shows the open guitar strings, their letter names, and their standard notation. The guitar always sounds one octave lower than the notes written on the staff. Clicking the Help button provides instructions.

The vertical lines on the fingerboard are the strings, and the horizontal lines represent the frets. Clicking just above any fret simulates the placement of your finger on the fingerboard. When you click on a string, the notation is changed to reflect the sound of the guitar. When the notes you have entered make up a common musical chord, its label appears as shown above.

The check boxes above the strings stop the strings—that is, stopped strings are not played and their notes do not appear on the staff. When you click the Enter button, the musical structure is entered in the Triads or 7th Chords subject, and it displays the principal notes of your guitar chord.

The remaining pages of this appendix contain guitar chord charts with fingerings for playing those chords. An X above a string means that the string is not played in that chord. 0 means that the string is open—no finger is placed on the string. (0) means that the string's note fits into the chord but it is not generally played.

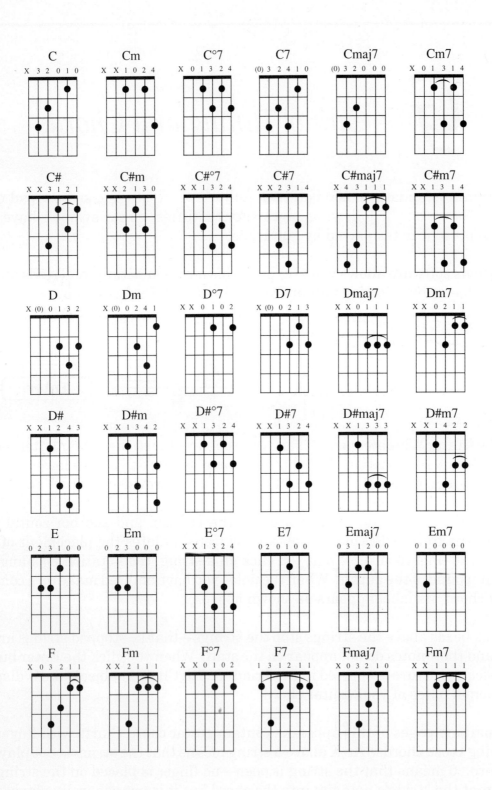

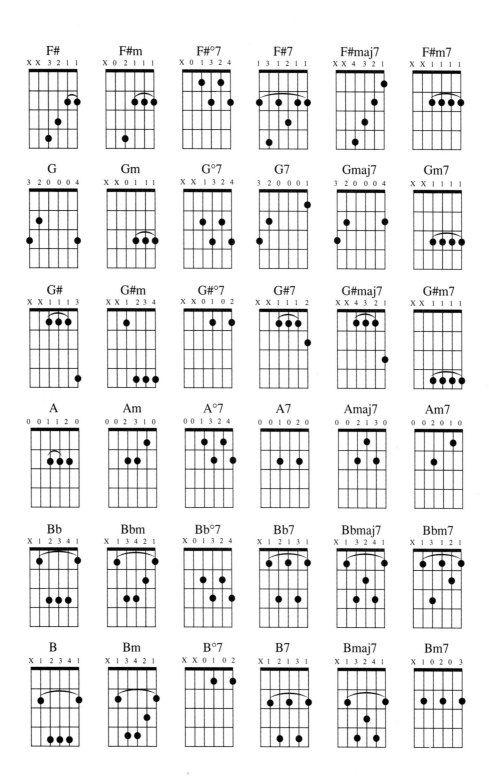

Use these blank chord charts to write other chords or alternative fingerings.

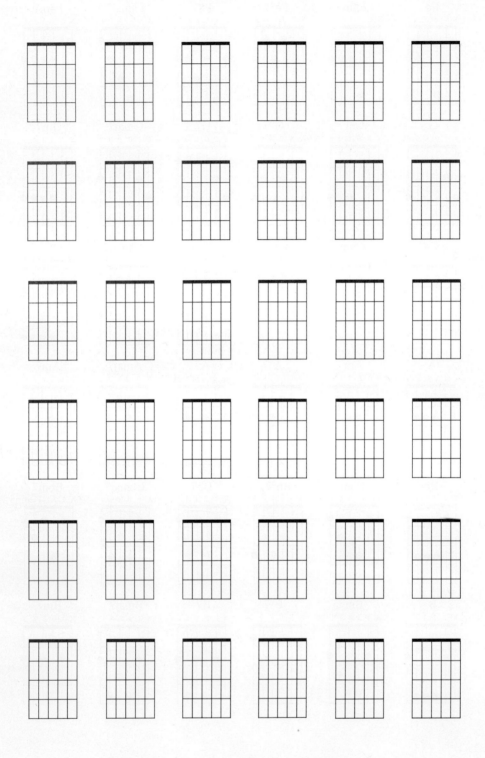

$\mathcal{H}$ Modal Scales

As you work within the Scales subject, *Explorations* software will analyze the scales you construct. At times modal scale terms will appear as you build various scales. For example, if you add a flat to the B in a C major scale, *Explorations* software will label that scale "C Mixolydian." Although a complete discussion of modal scales is beyond the scope of this book, this appendix contains examples of these scales. Modal scales are important structures, used in both ancient and modern music. Jazz musicians consider them very important for learning to construct melodies over chord progressions. Figure H–1 contains the modes as they were used in ancient music, starting on various notes of the staff. Figure H–2 shows these same scales, all transposed to C. Notice the similarities between the Ionian, Lydian, and Mixolydian modes. These are all similar to the major mode discussed in Chapter 5. The Dorian, Phrygian, and Aeolian modes all resemble the minor mode presented in Chapter 6. The ordering of the modes on C in Figure H–2 allows you to see this relationship clearly.

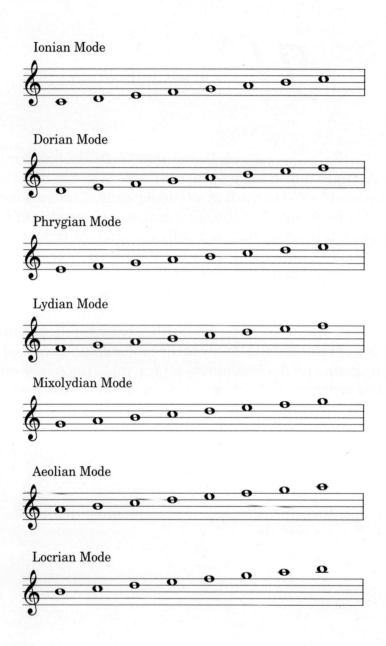

Figure H–1

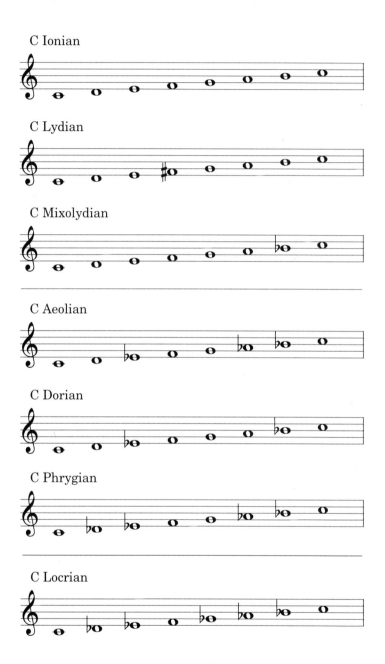

Figure H–2

Glossary

accent
Emphasis of a particular note because of its metric placement, dynamic level, accent marking, articulation, duration, or register.

accidental
A sign placed before a note to temporarily raise or lower its pitch or to cancel a previous accidental.

accompaniment
A portion of a musical texture that is designed to serve as a background, especially to support a melody.

amplitude
A measure of the difference in air pressure between compressions and rarefactions. The ear perceives this difference as loudness.

anacrusis
A single note or group of notes that form an incomplete measure before the first measure of a piece or section of a piece. These notes are also called **upbeats** or **pickups**.

arpeggiation
The presentation of chord tones one at a time. This often occurs in accompaniments of melodies. Melodies can arpeggiate chords as well.

asymmetrical meter
A meter in which the beats of the measure are units of five, seven, or eleven rather than equal units of two or three. Asymmetrical meters combine at least one group of two beats with at least one group of three beats.

authentic cadence
A cadence that consists of the dominant (V) and tonic (I) chords. The authentic cadence is the most common cadence in Western tonal music.

barline
A vertical line that extends from the top to the bottom of the staff and marks the beginning or ending of a measure.

bass
Pronounced "bayss"
1) The lowest male voice type. This term is applied to both soloists and choral singers.
2) The name given to a string bass or electric bass used in small combos.
3) The term is also used to refer to the lowest voice of any multiple-voice musical composition.

beam
A solid, wide line that combines two or more notes with a rhythmic value less than a quarter note.

beat
The basic pulse of a musical composition. Beats are most often organized in groups of two (duple) and three (triple).

boom-chick
A musical texture characterized by a bass note followed later by a chord above. This combination is repeated over and over using various chords.

cadence
A point in the music where rhythmic, melodic, and harmonic elements combine to give a sense of repose. This is often created through a slowing or break in musical motion and serves as a punctuation between phrases.

canon
Another word for round: a musical composition in which all voices sing the same music but at different times. The "leader" starts the canon and each "follower" starts with the same music after the appropriate length of time. "Row, Row, Row Your Boat" and "Are You Sleeping?" are popular canons, or rounds.

chorale
A hymn tune that originated in the Lutheran Church during the sixteenth century. A famous set of harmonizations of chorale melodies was written by J. S. Bach in the eighteenth century. Each chorale includes several stanzas of verse, all of which are sung to the same music.

chord	A musical structure made up of three or more different pitches (not counting octave duplications). Chords can be played as a simultaneous group of notes. They can also be implied by a melody line that plays the notes of the chord one at a time.
chordal	A term describing a type of texture in which all parts move with the same rhythms, producing a succession of harmonies.
chromatic	A term describing music where the notes are not confined to the pitches of a diatonic scale. For example, the diatonic notes of C major are C, D, E, F, G, A, and B. Any other notes (e.g., F#, Db) are considered chromatic.
chromatic scale	The scale formed by all twelve pitches of the octave, arranged in ascending or descending order.
clef	A sign placed at the left side of a musical staff that indicates which pitches will be represented by the lines and spaces.
common tone	A tone that is a member of two different chords. For example, C is a common tone between the C major and F major triads.
common-tone model	A method for voice leading between adjacent chords with a root progression of an ascending fourth where the common tone between the two chords is held or iterated in a single voice.
compound interval	An interval that is larger than an octave. Ninths, tenths, etc. are compound intervals. Ninths, elevenths, and thirteenths are the compound intervals used most often in discussing music. The others are described by saying "an octave and a _____." A twelfth is an octave and a fifth.
compound meter	A meter in which the primary division of the beat is in three parts (triple). 6/8, 9/8, and 12/8 are the most common compound meter time signatures.
compression	In the cycle of a sound wave, the point at which the air pressure is higher than it would normally be in the absence of a sound wave. The air molecules are compressed together. On a graphic representation of sound, compression is shown in the higher points of the waveform.
cycle	A term used to identify one complete occurrence of a compression and rarefaction of the air molecules in a sound wave. At least twenty cycles per second must take place in order for a sound to be audible by humans. Regular recurring cycles produce sounds with a frequency. From all frequencies certain pitches are chosen to make music.
data bytes	In a stream of MIDI data, numbers between zero and 127 which describe notes or settings associated with the operative status byte. For example, when a Note-on command is sent by a synthesizer, there are always two data bytes that follow. These are the number of the note played and the velocity with which the key was depressed.
deceptive cadence	Also called an interrupted cadence. A cadence that occurs where an authentic cadence is expected and consists of a dominant (V) chord followed by a sub-mediant (vi) chord.
diatonic	A term referring to music or intervals confined to the pitch material of a given scale or mode. Major and minor scales are diatonic scales.
diminished seventh chord	A diminished triad plus an interval of a diminished seventh above its root. This chord most often occurs on the leading tone of a minor key.
dominant	The functional name given to the fifth degree of a major or minor scale or to the triad formed on this pitch. The chord based on this scale degree is almost always major and combines with the tonic chord to establish a key.
dominant preparation	Chords that prepare the listener for the arrival of the dominant (V). Supertonic and subdominant chords are the most common dominant preparation chords.

dominant seventh chord	The seventh-chord type formed on the dominant scale degree. It consists of a major triad with a minor seventh above its root. This type of seventh chord appears diatonically only on the dominant (fifth scale degree).
dot	A sign placed after a note or rest that increases its duration by one-half of the original value. For example, a dotted quarter note is equal to three eighth notes. The original quarter note is equivalent to two eighth notes. Its value is increased by half (one eighth note) by adding a dot to the note.
double flat ♭♭	A symbol that, placed before a note on a staff, lowers its pitch by two half steps. The double-flatted note is played two keyboard keys to the left of its unaltered position.
double sharp ✕	A symbol that, placed before a note on a staff, raises its pitch by two half steps. The double-sharped note is played two keyboard keys to the right of its unaltered position.
duple meter	A meter in which the beats are grouped two to a measure. 2/4 is a simple duple meter. 6/8 is a compound duple meter.
duplet	A note value used in compound meters that divides a length of time into two parts. For example, a dotted quarter note value can be divided into two duplet dotted eighth notes. Normally the dotted quarter note would be divided into three eighth notes in compound meters.
duration	The length of a note. Rhythmic values (eighth notes, quarter notes, and so forth), in conjunction with the Tempo, indicate the duration of a note.
dynamics	Markings and words used to indicate the relative levels of loudness or softness of a musical segment.
enharmonic	A term describing different spellings of the same pitch. For example, D♯ and E♭ are enharmonic notes.
entry window	A window in *Explorations* software that allows the user to select musical labels and enter them as requests to see a musical structure or as answers to questions in practice sessions and tests.
final	The principal tone of a mode, usually the tone upon which melodies in the mode end. It is similar to the tonic in major and minor scales.
first inversion	Any arrangement of the tones of a triad or seventh chord in which the third of the chord appears as the lowest pitch.
flag	A curved line added to the stem of single notes with a rhythmic value less than a quarter note.
flat ♭	A symbol that, placed before a note on a staff, lowers its pitch by one half step. The flatted note is played one keyboard key to the left of its unaltered position.
follower	See Canon.
frequency	The rate of a periodic vibration, usually expressed as a number of cycles per second.
fundamental	The lowest (and usually the loudest) tone in a harmonic series. It is produced by a body (e.g., a string or air column) vibrating in its entirety.
grand staff	A treble clef staff and bass clef staff, combined with a brace or bracket on their left side, on which keyboard music is notated.
half cadence	A cadence that ends on a dominant (V) chord. This chord is normally preceded by a subdominant (IV) or supertonic (ii) chord.
half-diminished seventh chord	The chord formed by combining a diminished triad with a minor seventh above its root. This chord appears diatonically on the leading tone (vii°) of a major key and on the supertonic (ii°) of a minor key.
half step	The smallest interval normally used in Western music and the smallest interval on the piano keyboard. It is the distance from any keyboard key to the next key regardless of color.

harmonic	1) A term generally used to refer to the effect of several musical lines in combination. Chords are the building blocks of harmony. 2) In acoustics, a frequency component in a periodic waveform that exists above the fundamental.
harmonic function	The role that a chord plays in a given key. Each chord plays a role in establishing a strong key center. For example, a dominant chord generally resolves to a tonic chord to establish key. Supertonic and subdominant chords lead to the dominant and are often called dominant preparation chords. These functions are derived from common practice of composers and are labeled using roman numerals.
harmonic intervals	Intervals that occur between notes that sound simultaneously.
harmonic minor scale	The natural minor scale with the seventh degree raised by one half step. This forms a leading tone to the tonic note. It is the form most often used to build chords in minor keys.
harmonic series	The spectrum of frequencies that are present in the sound along with the fundamental. These frequencies are whole-number multiples of the fundamental frequency and are responsible for giving a sound its timbre, or tone color.
harmony	The effect produced by the simultaneous sounding of several pitches. Chords, such as triads and seventh chords, are common harmony structures.
hemiola	A particular type of 3:2 rhythmic ratio involving divisions of six rhythmic values into three groups of two values in contradiction to an assumed two groups of three values. One such division can follow the other or they can occur simultaneously.
hertz	A unit designating one cycle per second of a periodic waveform. Twenty hertz (20 Hz) = twenty cycles per second.
homophonic	A musical texture where one line is the most important and the others have a supporting role. Homophonic styles most often have the same rhythm present in all voices. Most hymns are homophonic.
interval	The distance between two pitches. Interval labels have two parts: the interval number specifies the number of staff positions between the written notes, and the interval quality is determined by the number of half steps present between the pitches.
inversion	1) Octave transposition of one of the pitches of an interval so that the lower pitch becomes the higher pitch and vice versa. 2) Any position of a triad or seventh chord in which the root is not the lowest voice.
iteration	The repetition of a single note.
key signature	A compilation of flats or sharps used consistently within a composition or within a section of a composition. These accidentals are written in a group immediately after the clef sign at the beginning of each staff.
leader	See Canon.
leading tone	The functional name of the seventh scale degree, which is a minor second below the tonic (e.g., F# in G major or G minor). This term is also used to label the diminished triad based on the seventh scale degree.
leap	A term used to describe a melodic skip of greater than one staff position.
ledger lines	Short horizontal lines that extend the staff in order to notate pitches too high or too low to be placed directly on the staff. Each line is drawn through the stem of each note and through the note head when the note is on a line.
legato	Smoothly, connected. A manner of performing music in which the notes are connected with little or no separation between them.

major scale	A scale made up of seven different notes with the interval pattern of whole step, whole step, half step, whole step, whole step, whole step, half step. This scale is normally written over the span of one octave with the first note (the tonic) written again at the octave.
major seventh chord	The chord formed by the addition of a major seventh above the root of a major triad. It is most often found on the tonic (I) and subdominant (IV) of a major key and on the submediant (VI) and mediant (III) of a minor key.
measure	An area of a staff specified by barlines that contains one complete set of the accent patterns established by the meter (time signature).
mediant	The functional name given to the third degree of a major or minor scale or to the triad formed on this pitch.
melodic intervals	Intervals formed between notes that follow one another in a piece.
melodic minor scale	A type of minor scale with two forms. The ascending form uses the tones of the natural minor scale but with the sixth and seventh degrees raised by one half step. The descending melodic minor is made up of the same notes as the natural minor scale. The melodic minor is the form on which melodies in the minor mode are most often based.
melody	A melody is a succession of pitches and durations that form a recognizable, linear musical unit. The melody of a composition can occur in any instrument or voice but is found most often in the highest musical line. Secondary notes performed as a background to the melody are called the accompaniment.
menu bar	The labels listed at the top of a Macintosh screen that indicate which menus are available to the user. The Apple, File, Edit, and Subject menus are always available to *Explorations* users. When a subject is selected from the Subject menu, an additional menu appears showing appropriate selections for that chosen subject.
meter	A regularly recurring pattern of strong and weak pulses or beats. The meter is the background against which a composition's rhythms are performed. Generally, when a group of rhythms is very similar to the steady pulse of the background meter, the musical composition is considered rhythmically uninteresting. When rhythms are varied and contrast with the meter, the composition tends to be more interesting.
middle C	The C key that is closest to the middle of a piano keyboard. It is the lowest note of MIDI octave 4 and is MIDI key number 60.
MIDI	The Musical Instrument Digital Interface. An industry standard for transmitting musical performance data between synthesizers and computers. The specification includes a standard hardware configuration and a standard protocol for sending data. For more information, see the MIDI Manufacturers Association web site, http://www2.midi.org/mma/. Send electronic mail to mma@midi.org.
minor scale	A scale whose original form (natural minor) is made up of seven different notes with the interval pattern of whole step, half step, whole step, whole step, half step, whole step, whole step. This scale is normally written over the span of one octave with the first note (the tonic) written again at the octave. Other forms of the minor mode have alterations added by the composer that produce other whole-step/half-step patterns. (See also Melodic minor and Harmonic minor.)
minor seventh chord	The chord formed by the addition of a minor seventh above the root of a minor triad. It is most often found on the supertonic of a major key and on the subdominant of a minor key.
modes	A set of scales that formed the basis of much medieval and Renaissance

music, predating the major and minor scales. These scales were used in concert music early in the twentieth century. They are still used in jazz compositions today.

monophonic Music in any style that consists of a single melodic line. Early forms of music (before 1000 A.D.) and certain folk music styles are monophonic.

musical texture The aural quality of the "surface" of a musical composition. Methods are used to compose out chords into rhythmic patterns that are associated with musical styles. Examples include arpeggiated textures and "boom-chick" figures.

Music Toolbox A group of icons beneath the menu bar in *Explorations* software that allow the user to select musical tools for entering music notation. Notation entry can be used to write compositions with the Music Editor or to enter the answers to questions in practice sessions and tests. A Play button is also included for playing any musical score present in the Subject Window.

natural ♮ A sign placed before a note that cancels the effect of any sharp or flat previously associated with that note. The natural restores the pitch to its unaltered state. All notes with naturals are played on white keys of the piano keyboard.

natural minor scale A seven-tone scale with the interval pattern of whole step, half step, whole step, whole step, half step, whole step, whole step. The notes of a natural minor scale are specified by its key signature.

noise An acoustical term used to describe sounds that have no periodic waveform, for example, the sound of a snare drum. It is also a word that is used commonly to describe unwanted sounds. This second usage has little place in the discussion of musical sound. Because the sound of a snare drum has no periodic waveform, it is considered a noise. However, we use such noises in music to excellent effect and aesthetic ends.

nonchord tone A tone that is not part of the prevailing harmony. These tones embellish the presence of the prevailing chord and often extend its presence over a longer period of time. They are also called nonharmonic tones.

non-common-tone model A method for voice leading between adjacent chords with a root progression of an ascending fourth where the common tone between the two chords is *not* held or iterated in a single voice.

note A sign used on a staff to represent the pitch and duration of a musical tone.

octave An interval of twelve half steps, from a given pitch to the next higher or lower pitch of the same letter name. The frequency ratio between two such pitches is 2:1. For example, an A-440 (440 cycles per second) is used to tune orchestras. The violins play this frequency on their open A string. The open A string of the cellos is one octave lower and has a frequency of 220.

overtone Any of the harmonics occurring above the fundamental frequency. (See Appendix C.)

parallel major/minor A major and a minor scale that share the same tonic. For example, C major and C minor are parallel major and minor.

periodic In acoustics, a term describing a repeating waveform. Fixed musical tones are generated by periodic waveforms.

phrase A melodic unit that presents a more or less complete musical thought. Phrases are typically four to eight measures long.

pickup See Anacrusis.

pitch The highness or lowness of a musical tone, which is the result of the frequency of a periodic waveform. A note is the graphic image of a pitch. The pitch is the specific frequency represented by a note. For example, it is generally agreed that the note on the second space of the treble staff should have a frequency of 440 cycles per second.

plagal cadence   A cadence consisting of the subdominant (IV) and tonic (I) chords.

polyphonic   A texture made up of two or more independent melodic lines. This is in contrast to a monophonic style, which consists of a single melodic line.

pop chord symbols   A system of symbols for labeling the quality of triads and seventh chords. These are often used with lead sheets to indicate which chords should be played with a melody. (See Appendix E.)

progression   1) Harmonic motion, which in most cases follows the series of ascending fourth root movements. Harmonic progression often generates a satisfying feeling of forward momentum.
2) A standard series of chords that are recognized as common among many musical compositions. For example, blues progressions in jazz compositions.

pulse   A regularly recurring stress to which we physically respond in spite of the rhythmic values of a work. These rhythmic values are measured in terms of the background pulse or beat. In simple meters, the term *pulse* is usually synonymous with beat. In compound meters, three pulses usually equal one beat.

quadruple meter   A meter in which the beats are grouped four to a measure. 4/4 and 12/8 are examples of quadruple meter.

rarefaction   The point in the cycle of a sound wave where the air pressure is less than the normal air pressure. Normal air pressure exists when air molecules are not disturbed by a sound wave.

relative major/minor   A major and a minor scale that share the same key signature. For example, D major and B minor share a key signature with two sharps.

repetition   The restatement of any musical idea. Individual notes, single chords, phrases, or large sections of a work can be repeated. Repetition does not have to be exact in order to be recognized as a restatement of musical material. Repeated chords can be revoiced. Repeated melodies can be embellished. Jazz improvisation on a given tune is a type of varied repetition of the original melody.

resolution   The motion from a tone or chord to another tone or chord of greater stability. For example, the leading tone tends to resolve to the tonic, providing an important feature in establishing a key.

rest   A time of silence in a composition or individual melodic line.

rhythm   The duration of the sounds and silences in a musical composition. Rhythms are generally performed against a metric background established by a time signature. The meter provides the basic pulse or beat for a composition.

roman numerals   Numeric symbols of scale degrees and chord quality used for music analysis. These symbols indicate the quality and the function of a chord within the prevailing key.

root   In a triad or seventh chord, the note above which the other notes can be arranged. Other chord members are the third, fifth, and seventh.

root position   Any arrangement of the tones of a chord in which the root appears as the lowest pitch.

root progression   The interval between the roots of two adjacent chords. Root progressions fall into three groups: root fourths and fifths, thirds, and seconds.

scale   An ordering of pitches consistently used in a musical composition. These notes are written in ascending or descending order. Each scale has a set of relationships based on half steps and whole steps between adjacent scale members. Each note in a major or minor scale has a particular scale degree.

scale degree	A position within a scale described by a number or term. Scale degrees are numbered one through eight. The terms *tonic, supertonic, mediant, subdominant, dominant, submediant,* and *leading tone* are used for scale degrees one through seven. Tonic is used to describe the repetition of the first scale degree an octave above. Scale degrees function together to establish key (see Chapters 10 and 13).
screen keyboard	A graphic image of a piano keyboard that can be used on the screen of *Explorations* software. It can be played by clicking the keys with the Pointer Tool. The software responds in the same manner as when notes are played on a MIDI keyboard.
second inversion	Any arrangement of the tones of a triad or seventh chord in which the fifth of the chord appears as the lowest pitch.
seventh chord	A four-note chord made up of triad (root, third, and fifth) plus a seventh above the root. The five principal qualities of seventh chords are: **major** - major triad, major seventh; **minor** - minor triad, minor seventh; **dominant** - major triad, minor seventh; **half-diminished** - diminished triad, minor seventh; **diminished** - diminished triad, diminished seventh.
sharp ♯	A symbol that, placed before a note on a staff, raises its pitch by one half step. The sharped note is played one keyboard key to the right of its unaltered position.
simple interval	An interval whose span is an octave or less.
simple meter	A meter in which the primary division of each beat is into two parts (duple).
slur	A curved line placed above or below two or more notes that are to be performed in a legato fashion (smoothly connected).
solfège	Also called solfeggio. A system to label degrees of a scale with the syllables do, re, mi, fa, sol, la, and ti. These syllables are used to sing melodies and associate the sound of a note or scale degree with each syllable. Fixed Do solfège always associates do with C, re with D, etc. Movable Do solfège associates do with the tonic of each major key, re with the supertonic, etc. Do-based minor solfège uses do as the tonic of the minor key and alters the third, sixth, and seventh scale degrees to me, le, and te. La-based minor solfège uses la as the tonic of the minor key.
soprano	1) The highest female voice type. This term is applied to both soloists and choral singers. 2) The term is also used to refer to the highest voice of any multiple-voice musical composition.
sound wave	A series of air pressure changes caused by a vibrating object. These changes hit the eardrum and are transmitted to the brain and interpreted as sound.
staff	A set of five horizontal lines used for notating music. Notes and other graphic symbols are written on and between these lines. A clef sign indicates the pitches associated with each line and space of the staff.
staff position	Each line on a staff and each space between lines. Notes "on a line" have a staff line running through them. Notes "in a space" are positioned between two lines.
status bytes	In a stream of MIDI data, numbers from 128($80) through 255($FF) which indicate MIDI commands. These numbers indicate the nature of the musical performance activity taking place, for example, playing notes, moving pitch wheels, or changing sounds.
step or stepwise	Melodic movement from one staff position to an adjacent staff position. No leaps.

subdivision	Just as measures are divided into beats, each beat has a common subdivision implied by the time signature. In simple meters the implied subdivision of each beat is duple. In compound meters the implied subdivision of each beat is triple.
subdominant	The functional name given to the fourth degree of a major or minor scale or to the triad formed on this pitch. For example, the F major triad is the subdominant of the key of C major. The F minor triad is the subdominant of the key of C minor.
Subject Window	The window in *Explorations* software that contains musical scores relating to each subject. This window also contains buttons for manipulating the format of these scores.
submediant	The functional name given to the sixth degree of a major or minor scale or to the triad formed on this pitch. For example, the A minor triad is the submediant of the key of C major. The A♭ major triad is the submediant of the key of C minor.
supertonic	The functional name given to the second degree of a major or minor scale or to the triad formed on this pitch. For example, the D minor triad is the supertonic of the key of C major. The D diminished triad is the supertonic of the key of C minor.
swing	A method of playing music written in simple meter to make it sound as if it was written in compound meter.
syncopation	The shift of accent to a portion of a beat or measure that is not normally accented.
tempo	The speed of the regular pulse or beat. Tempo is indicated generally by such words as allegro, andante, and so on. It can also be established by means of a diagram that shows a rhythmic value (quarter note, eighth note, etc.) followed by an equals sign and a number. This method indicates the number of such rhythmic values that should occur each minute.
theme	A musical idea, usually a melody, that forms the basis or starting point for a musical work.
third inversion	Any arrangement of the tones of a seventh chord in which the seventh of the chord appears as the lowest pitch.
tie	A curved line connecting two adjacent notes of the same pitch. In such cases the second note is not articulated. Instead, the two notes are combined into a single sound equal to their combined durations.
timbre	A term referring to the quality of a musical tone (tone color), which is determined by overtone content and the relative strengths of the overtones.
time signature	A two-digit numerical indication of the meter of a piece. Generally, the upper note indicates the number of beats per measure and the lower number indicates the type of note that gets one beat.
tonal	A term used to describe music in which a particular pitch is given greater importance and sense of finality than the other pitches.
tone	A term used to describe sounds with specific frequencies or pitches.
tonic	The first and most stable pitch of a given major or minor scale and the pitch for which the scale is named. This term is also used to describe the chord built on this scale degree.
transposition	The process of rewriting a scale, or a passage based on a scale, at a different pitch level. All intervallic and harmonic relationships remain consistent at the new pitch level.
triad	A three-note chord made up of a root (the tone on which the chord is based), a third (the tone a third above the root), and a fifth (the tone a fifth above the root).

triple meter	A meter in which the beats are grouped three to a measure. 3/4 and 9/8 are examples of triple meter.
triplet	A note value used in simple meters that divides a length of time into three parts. For example, a quarter note value can be divided into three triplet eighth notes. Normally the quarter note would be divided into two eighth notes in simple meters.
upbeat	See Anacrusis.
variation	A varied repetition of a musical idea, involving the modification of rhythmic, melodic, harmonic, or timbral changes of the musical material. Variation is most often associated with melodic changes but can be based on a series of chords upon which one improvises.
vibration	A periodic repetition of compressions and rarefactions, that is, regularly occuring disturbances of air which produce sound.
voice leading	The ways in which voices commonly move horizontally when the harmony changes.
voicing	The vertical distribution of chord notes among the various voices of a musical texture.
whole step	An interval comprising two half steps.

Index